The Great Canadian Woman

She is Strong and Free

Sarah Swain
and 13 Inspiring Co-Authors

For permission requests, write to The Great Canadian Woman at:
team@thegreatcanadianwoman.ca

Published by Prominence Publishing
www. Prominencepublishing.com

Quantity sales. Special discounts are available on quantity purchases by corporations, associations, and others. For details, contact The Great Canadian Woman head office at the address above.

ISBN 978-1-9992151-0-1

A Note to the Reader

Before you open the pages of this book, we need to have a conversation.

I wrestled with myself on whether or not to proceed with the publication of this book.

This isn't a PR stunt. This is my truth.

When I started The Great Canadian Woman podcast, I had no idea the magnitude of responsibility I had taken on, simply by assuming the name of the brand itself. I remember texting with my sister about the fears I had about taking on the brand name, because I could feel the responsibility of it although I didn't know why. All I know is that it felt bigger than me. She was quick to dish out a mini-lecture about fear, similar to the ones I had given to her in the past to help her navigate through adversity and build belief in herself. Touché, little sis'.

As I launched the podcast on July 1st, 2018, I knew something big had just landed in Canada, but I couldn't put a finger on why it felt as big as it did. And over time, as a community began to form around the podcast, I started to recognize that others felt it too. Big. Powerful. Resounding. Proud. These were all words that started circulating when people experienced The Great Canadian Woman. There was a powerful, yet silent connection that people were starting to feel. It was both exhilarating, and terrifying as the weight of the responsibility started to grow on top of my shoulders.

On International Women's Day 2019, The Great Canadian Woman podcast was featured by Apple Podcasts as part of their Inspiring Women campaign. I burst into tears of gratitude when I got the notification, because it was just 2 years prior that I voiced my own concerns about the lack of focus that the organization had on the development of women within our place of work. I was fired up, but I was also solution based and offered to head up a Diversity Committee to help move the needle forward for the organization. Although my solution was deferred, I was proud that I rocked the boat and got people thinking. Which brings me back to why I wrestled with myself on whether or not to proceed with the publication of this book.

While this book represents communities such as womanhood, mental health, addictions recovery, victims of homicide, the disabled, motherhood, and many others, this book doesn't represent the deep culture and diversity of Canada. I recognize this, and I wrestled with proceeding with this book for this very reason. Despite my attempts at a diverse author base from the beginning, and having lost a few authors along the way as we moved from one publishing house to another, we arrived at the finish line with the 14 incredible women you will read about in this book. These women are some of the strongest women I have encountered and their stories moved me at a cellular level. As a result, I was unwilling to rob them of the opportunity to share their stories and impact and touch the hearts of so many people across the country, simply because I, as the leader, didn't do more to diversify the platform right out of the gates. We are growing, and I am learning.

So it is my hope that I am met with compassion, understanding and better yet – assistance. I am asking for help. I am committed to this process, to learning and to growing in order to make all Canadian women feel welcome, included and accepted here in this space. Men, too! It is my sincerest hope that you will feel the interconnectedness across all stories in this book, as our stories truly are what connect us all.

As this is the first book of many in a series, I have onboarded a panel of advisors to serve as the Diversity committee for The Great Canadian Woman. Everything we create, publish and host will be fully discussed and rigorously vetted to ensure we meet the expectations of Canadians and do a really beautiful job of representing everyone who resonates with being a Canadian woman.

Deep breath. It is now that I ask you to turn the page, and allow yourself to experience the beauty, the strength, the power and the inspiration that exists in the pages of this book.

In gratitude,
Sarah Swain
Owner, Founder
The Great Canadian Woman Inc.

Contents

Introduction

We can be pretty tough on ourselves for not feeling the way we think we should feel, not doing the things we think we should be doing, not following the plan we think we should be following, not learning more, not knowing better, not leaping sooner, not healing faster - and the list goes on. We become so used to flowing with the current and the raging rapids it brings with it, that the mere thought of making any attempt at turning around and swimming upstream is unfathomable. The standard response is to go with the flow and ride the waves and make the best of it, hoping we don't feel too much more pain on the way down, hoping that at some point things will get better and the waters will become calm.

Some raise their hand in search of a branch to latch on-to to pull themselves out.

Some lean onto the rocks that stand sturdy, so they can regain their energy and regroup.

Some open their eyes to all that surrounds them and take an inventory of their total environment.

Some survey the land in order to decide what to do next, where, how and with whom.

Some trust themselves enough to carve out a path on their own.

Some know deep down, that there is another option.

These women.

Trailblazer *(noun)* - a person who makes, does, or discovers something new and makes it acceptable or popular. A woman who has quarreled with the depths of pain and treacherous misalignment in life has two options to choose from. Hard, or harder. Does she choose hard and move forward in the face of uncertainty with the slightest hope that there may be a light at the end of the tunnel? Or does she choose harder by staying where she is, in the certainty of her fears, pain, frustration and shame?

These women epitomize the strength that we all possess within, yet few believe to be true. With a fierce combination of willpower, determination, love and hope, they rose their heads up above the raging waters. Some used every last bit of their energy to turn around and swim upstream in an act of blind faith that inner peace would be on the horizon. Some crawled ashore and collected themselves before climbing the inevitable mountains that stood tall in the path to their personal freedom. And some carved and created the necessary tools to whack the brush and weeds out of their way to achieve happiness and fulfillment. These women made waves, moved mountains and blazed trails, and they have come together to share their stories, to ignite a spark within you; a spark that lights up just enough space in the darkness to show you what's possible for you, too. I assure you, the purported superpowers that each of these women emanate, exist within you, too. Whether you feel stuck in relationships that don't serve your highest self, toil with the confusing landscape of mental health, struggle to navigate the tsunami of grief, are face to face with demons of addictions, lack certainty in your self-worth, or are on a journey through adversity with your physical health - you will find it within you to stand strong and free.

And so she learned how to care without compromising her truth.
She learned her voice was the sound she wanted in her head when
the day came to an end.
She was not a shelving system for others to place their worries and
cares into.
Make no mistake,
Her heart was always open,
She was a pillar that many could lean on.
It was her manner,
Her instinct,
Her ability to choose self-forgiveness,
Self-compassion,
Self-awareness,
Self-worth,
That had the biggest and most significant impact for the community she served.
She was a leader not because she was appointed,
It was her story that honoured her this title.
She had faced the demons of the world and the demons in her mind
and instead of succumbing to the evil,
She chose instead to rise.
She chose to smile,
To laugh with tears in her eyes,
To whisper final goodbyes,
To not let the cruel happenings take out her light.
The Great,
The humbly Canadian,
The Women who have found the melody of freedom and peace inside.

−Cassie Jeans

IG: @cassie_mjeans

FAITH

Faith defies all logic, it doesn't make sense and it doesn't need to. It is that deep, impenetrable feeling we grab a hold of when there is little to no evidence around us to support what we hope to come true. It exists deep within our soul and extends far beyond the depth of what it means to simply believe. Faith is the sole morsel of comfort we find solace in as we lie awake at night fighting off what haunts us in our consciousness. It consoles us when the fear, worry and grief feels all too consuming and it keeps us company when everyone else has seemed to have given up or moved on. It is the root of our prayers, even when we have lost hope in who or what we are even praying to. Like a shawl we adorn ourselves in for comfort on a cool autumn evening, we wrap ourselves in our Faith for comfort, so we can hang on just a little longer.

Jessica's story epitomizes the power of never losing faith, despite everything staring back at her in her environment suggesting that she should. This is the journey of a mother's addictions through the eyes of her daughter, and through this powerful story, Jessica proves that Faith is what gives birth to miracles.

"If only she could escape his grasp, she'd find an unfathomable life beyond his walls of limitation.

If only she could escape her captor of addiction."

–Jessica De Castro

CHAPTER ONE

Heroin's Child

As consciousness creeps in, it finds her eyelids heavy. The first thing that meets her is darkness. Caution peeks as she tries to remember where she is. The breeze as cold as the floor beneath her, she reaches around to discover an asphalt road beyond her blanket. As her eyes adjust to the dark, a vaguely familiar laneway makes an appearance. Although mildly comforting, barely indicating, as laneways are abundant in Toronto and many are her friend. The sound of birds chirping is anxiety's cue - a signal that day is near. She's grown so comfortable with the night. As she rubs her arms to rid the chill, she feels a pain which she pays no mind. The fresh marks and swelling are nothing alarming, they trace the fleeting moments of numbness that drift her away from self-hatred and fear. As she begins to rise and gather what little she has, she releases the hope of remembering how she ended up here. Towards no particular destination, she walks until she's met by her reflection in a large garage window. She often forgets about the bruises that frequent her face until she's forced to confront herself. She looks away. The blink of surprise as swift as the change in pace, as predictable as the new destination in mind. The numbness never lasts quite long enough.

(Q

By six years old I had put enough pieces together to know what kind of sickness my mom had. When I'd lay down and close my eyes, I could feel her presence and embody her fear. I'd imagine I was her – feeling her emotions, experiencing her pain, torturing myself with worry. The dark thoughts would follow me like shadows, patiently waiting for moments of too much happiness. How could I be happy if she was so sad? How could I have friends if she was alone? The guilt nagged at me relentlessly. Her absence riddled me with questions. Even her occasional letters in the mail would be sealed with the guilt that I was going on without her.

Every time the phone rang, I anticipated my mother's voice. I longed for the operator who would say I had "a collect call from Daisy". My family warned me not to ac-cept the charges, but I didn't listen. I didn't know that her collect calls came from jail or that they were likely bearers of bad news. When we'd get the chance to talk, she kept it positive, attempting to paint a certain kind of picture. She'd say, "See you soon," though I rarely would. This routine was the art of our relationship, with delicate brush strokes concealing the mistakes, the splatters of lies, the blotches of reality. It turns out, she wasn't the only one holding a brush. Everyone seemed to have one.

My family wanted to protect me, wishing I could exist only within the frame of childhood where I wouldn't have to worry about my mother. At the core, it didn't matter what my mother called for, or where she called from. I just wanted to hear from her, to know she was Ok. I'd always hear people say she was going to die soon. That she was bound to overdose somewhere outside the lines. So naturally, the sound of her voice served as the tiniest brush strokes of comfort that perhaps her story wouldn't have the outcome they were expecting.

Elementary school was challenging as a chubby girl with a big personality. The fact that everyone knew all the personal details of my life didn't help. Although this was partly because I sought comfort through people's pity, it was heavily aided by our European community's enslavement to gossip. My refuge from all that wasn't right, was my aunt; Tia Paula. Her love was my safe space. Being my legal and spiritual guardian, she took the time to care for me like no one else. I was in her custody with the support of my maternal grandparents for as long as I could remember. I had other aunts, uncles, cousins and two incredible father figures that all brightened my dark days. But overpowering the abundance of external love that I received from them, was the lack of internal love I had for myself. Amidst my physical and silent weight, the feelings of abandonment sitting like rocks in my stomach and all the self doubt, bulimia became an easy coping mechanism and dangerous friend. It awarded me with an immense relief that I didn't understand to be detrimental in any way, and I went a long time without anyone knowing that anything was wrong. I had great school counsellors who tried their best to help me manage my emotions but could never seem to calm my aggressively expressive personality or my temper for when all that the emotions took a bad turn. Passionate to a fault, I was always on the defence for myself and others. This often led to verbal and physical altercations that earned me a lot of time in detention, yet the peak of the rollercoaster never seemed to near.

Recess in my memory has seemed to blur into one long day of playing red-ass and hopscotch. There are only a few moments that really stand out as individuals including my grade 3 marriage at the sand box, a last day of school water fight and this particularly vivid day. As I was playing in the school yard, I saw my mom standing at the fence with two men I didn't recognize. Fumbling to connect the bridge between panic and anticipation, I got it together and ran in her direction, hoping she'd miss my moment's doubt. I knew she wasn't allowed to visit me at school, but my heart ached for her. Seeing her felt like every emotion balled up in one. As we locked hands through the fence and talked, I noted the indicators of mumbled speech and awkward movements which made me uncomfortable. I knew what to look for by then and her entourage wasn't helping. They didn't dare make eye contact or break a smile, making their presence intolerable. Immediately after my mother left, I was approached by a male classmate who was quick to taunt, "Do you think your mom can sell me some crack?" Needless to say, that didn't go well for him. I suppose it didn't go well for me either as I ended up in the office yet again. Ironically, my mom's poor state nor the fight were what clouded my mind as I sat in detention. I'd lost my penny pendant during the fight.

It was one of the few gifts my mom had given me and I wore it religiously. After detention, I spent hours searching the yard and was consoled when I finally found it. I cried in relief as I squeezed it in my hands, holding it to my chest. This tiny pendant was my point of connection to Mom.

(Q

At the end of my Grade 1 school year, I found out I wouldn't be an only child anymore. My first reaction was fury. Erupting into the temper tantrum of my life, I thought of everything I'd have to share. Little did I know, I wouldn't be sharing much. When Kylie was born, I rarely saw her. After two shaky years with my mom and one long year in foster care, Kylie spent the next twelve years in the care of our cousin, then many on her own. Through all the instability life has thrown her way, her kind heart and loving nature has endured all. Four years later, my second sister entered the word. My mother was in the same sick state of mind and knew she wasn't Ok to take care of her either. Haley was immediately adopted by a family friend who couldn't have children of her own. She was happier than anyone I'd ever seen to be a mother.

Although I have deep bonds with my sisters, I often wish we had the opportunity to grow up like other siblings. I wish that I'd been at a closer distance to help them through their own struggles and relieve them of some of the burdens they carried. I wish I could have shared my knowledge, shared my love, shared myself, a little more. Because we grew up apart from each other, we missed out on a lot of things that siblings usually experience together. The divide wasn't easy, but we did our best, just like we do today.

Through all that transpired I couldn't empathise with my family's resentment towards my mother. I saw the drug abuse as a monster that had consumed her and believed wholeheartedly that her awareness of everything outside of her bubble didn't exist. Despite the helplessness I felt for my sisters and everyone involved, I knew in my heart my mom's intentions weren't malicious. I was passionately protective of her, often fighting with my family in her defense. The innocence in how I saw her was foreign to them. They lived through pain and betrayal that I couldn't fathom. She hadn't stolen my things and sold them for drugs. She hadn't taken advantage of my love with deceit and manipulation, yet. All I had was my own experiences, and I didn't want to lose faith like it seemed they had.

That unwavering belief in others came to a temporary halt in High School. As I navigated through adolescence, I learned many valuable lessons that presented themselves as heartaches. No matter how hard I tried to fit in, the reality was that I didn't. I wasn't like my peers. They didn't understand me. Making friends was easy and impossible all at the same time. Although striking up conversations and making myself known wasn't an issue, I struggled to form friendships that grew outside the school walls. Despite the deep, burning desire to build meaningful relationships with people, I was scared. The fear of people not liking me, at the depths of me. The fear of not being accepted. The fear of being pushed out. Fear controlled me. It told me that I wasn't worthy of the friendships that surrounded me. I expected people to let me down, so they did. The fear attracted all kinds of negative experiences. It was the law of attraction, not at its finest.

Relationships just weren't working for me, and I couldn't figure out why. When I started dating, those relationships didn't work either. In fact, they were pure chaos. I tried to use the control I didn't seem to have over my life, and the manipulation I'd learned from my mother, to get my way. When that didn't work for me, the failure of those relationships stripped more layers off my self worth. The boys my age were often thrill seekers, looking for any reason to party and any way to break the rules. I didn't care about their kind of parties, and I had no interest in breaking those rules. My grandmother always talked about staying clear of the "wrong path", yet those paths didn't always seem very clear. There wasn't a map to tell me where to go, and looking up at the sky didn't bring me any clarity. Even the sun that kept me warm, could blind me. I soon abandoned the thought of fitting in, and decided that no matter how difficult it was to not be accepted, that I would hang on to who I knew I wanted to be. My refusal to compromise my integrity isolated me. My strong view on drugs and alcohol didn't make me someone who got invited places with friends. People made me feel like I wasn't any fun because I wouldn't "let loose" and I believed it. I wished I could have friends who would explore new places with me. Friends who I could share my dreams with. I wanted to have game nights and go to concerts with no strings attached, but I couldn't find people who related. The conversations surrounding me were so out of line with who I was, that I slowly lost myself. I would have panic attacks so bad that I would black out. I would cry so hard that I would throw up, enjoying the physical pain of it because it felt like a punishment. My mindset was so twisted that I don't know how I got through my days. Hot showers and chamomile tea were comforting, but before I knew it, the weight of unalignment would swallow me again.

When I found out my mother was pregnant with my fourth sister, I was flooded with conflicting emotions. I was excited to have another sister to love, but scared about what would happen to her. At this point, my mother was in the worst shape she'd ever been. She was only thirty-two, but neglect had aged her. She'd just reappeared after a year-long disappearance, and was now living more than an hour away. She was completely and utterly broken in every sense. The day she called to tell us she was expecting, plays clear in my mind. I remember where I was standing in the house, what the room smelled like. I remember sitting down on the floor, picking pieces from the grey carpet, wondering, "What would happen to this baby? How could she do this to us again?" I couldn't possibly have the capacity to worry about anyone or anything else. I cried until I fell asleep, in the middle of that grey carpet, with the blanket of uncertainty smothering me.

When Destiny finally entered the world, she was six weeks premature. The whole situation was nerve wracking and it was all I could think about. After the first few weeks, despite all the odds being against them, there was a sudden shift. The only news coming in was good news. My sister was getting healthier every day, my mom was sounding clearer than ever and things were increasingly calm. I felt a little less anxious, a little less worried. It seemed Destiny had finally turned a kind eye mom's way.

Over the next few years, my mom began to build relationships with women who were also trying to improve their lives. They raised their kids together and pushed each other to grow and make better decisions. Even though things weren't always perfect, as a group, they persevered and having that support system, having genuine friends, made all the difference. I don't know what exactly it was that flipped the switch for my mom. I don't know if it was Destiny, her new friends, or the simplicity of just deciding she'd had enough. I don't know if it was the loss of her children, the estrangement from her family, or the will of fate that made the difference. Maybe it was a little bit of everything, but it didn't really matter. She now had the burning intention to be better, which meant she would be soon enough.

Eventually, she started joining us for holidays. I never imagined I'd ever have a holiday with everyone I loved in one room. Luckily, I was able to have a few of those perfect days. Days where everyone put their differences aside and appreciated the togetherness. On the contrary, there were some days I'd rather forget. One Christmas someone made a comment that was meant to put her down, and it did. Before I knew it she was screaming and sobbing, grabbing all her things, making her way for the door. Hyperventilating, I cried and pleaded for her not to leave. I grabbed her, dragging her back into the house by force because I didn't know what else to do. It suddenly felt like everything that had mended up until that point was falling apart and I knew I couldn't do it all over again. She tried to hit me, yelling in my face but I was bigger than her already. She dug her nails deep into my hands, drawing blood until I couldn't bear the pain and had to let her go. After such a turbulent flight, a near crash, the air smoothed. She didn't leave that night and we were able to get it together just in time to open gifts as if nothing had happened at all. I presume that time will draw lines amongst my veins, across the scars that grace my hands. I presume there will come a day that the marks blend into the signs of age and reside only in my memory. Another way that forgiveness and time can free us.

In hindsight, the addiction made the ups and downs inevitable. There were times where I feared a relapse loomed and there were times that one did. The recklessness of my mother's emotions got the best of her some days, with past traumas shaking up the stability. Nonetheless, she persisted and I was able to begin to relax and focus more on my own life. Her tenacity allowed her to persevere, breaking down all the roadblocks of PTSD and habit. It was as if she'd found something in herself that she thought was lost and it ignited a bravery and determination she didn't know she had within her.

If you met my mother today, you'd meet a strong minded, outspoken, and incredibly kind woman. She's the best version of herself I've had the chance to know. After being on methadone treatment for more than ten years, she's recently freed herself from that dependence too – another win. She calls me every day and I actually love talking to her. The positive development of our relationship has relieved me of a heavy pain I was holding on to. Experiencing this journey with her has taught me many invaluable lessons, but none more significant than having the compassion to give others the benefit of the doubt. You can never know the amount of courage someone holds in their heart. Once we break through the glass ceiling of our limiting beliefs, we inspire the same liberation in others. I hope you find some inspiration within the strength we found in ourselves.

In spring 2018, I found myself in church for a family occasion. Until my early teens, I prayed every night. My prayers were lengthy, a full conversation with God. I would list every person I cared about one by one, careful not to forget anyone. I made wishes for them in incredible detail, closing my eyes and visualizing as I prayed. Being back in church, I realized how long it had been since I'd felt that devotion. I'd convinced myself I wasn't welcome, that I didn't belong. As the priest spoke, I considered his words and reflected on what they meant and didn't mean to me now. When it was time to take the host, I followed my family, accepted the holy bread, and walked back to my seat. It was time to pray. Kneeling, I closed my eyes, and was hit with an indescribable sensation. I felt goosebumps take over my body. Tears burst from my eyes. I was inconsolable. I cried, drawing the attention of concerned family. Words could not escape my lips and I didn't know how to explain even if I tried. A massive realization had occurred to me. Every time I had ever gotten to this point in a mass, I had prayed for the same thing. I had prayed that my mom would be okay. That she would overcome her addiction. That she would have relationships with us. That her bond with my grandmother would be mended. And here I was, with all my prayers having come true, without ever fully taking in this miracle that happened before my eyes. I have never had a moment so awakening, so full of gratitude as that moment. Just pure gratitude.

CO

Rousing from her sleep, she takes consciousness by the hand. Her eyes meet the sunlight as it shines into her room. Calm surrounds her as she lays awake, feeling thankful for this sanctuary. The sun as warm as the blanket around her, she begins to rise, getting ready to greet the new day. While making her bed and arranging the pillows, she sees her big orange cat sneak into the room. The sound of her dogs barking is love to her ears - a reminder she's never alone here. As she makes her way to Destiny's room, she hears laughter that carries through the halls. She's grown comfortable in a full house. As she reaches the door, she isn't alarmed by the messy room and sleepless friends. She knows the fleeting moments of her teenage years will be missed one day. As they duck under the sheets and burst into giggles, she peacefully reminisces on a time she did this with her sisters. As she walks downstairs, her dogs come running, licking her ankles and wildly wagging their tails. Before entering the kitchen to make her coffee, she meets her reflection in the mirror. She smiles – she often forgets how much better she looks now that she's learning to love herself. The intention of a good day, as powerful as her perseverance, as real as this life. She feels free.

Acknowledgement: This piece is dedicated to my Mother, without whom there would be no story. To my Vavó, who kept me in line with her tough love. And to my Tia Paula, who supports me, believes in me and cares for me like no one else. I love you all more than these words could ever relay.

About the Author

Jessica's first love was the city of Toronto, where she grew up mesmerized by its diversity and vibrant atmosphere. Immersing herself into its culture and endless opportunities, she found an outlet for her pain through writing and the performing arts. Today, that same appreciation lives strong, as she continues to be inspired by the cultural harmony and individuality that the city embraces. Aside from Toronto, Jessica dreams to explore the rest of the world and create change for important causes from environmental sustainability and animal welfare, to government policies and societal norms. Jessica's creative mind and outside-the-box thinking are what make her a talented writer, powerful speaker and brilliant business leader. She has a niche for branding and understanding consumers which has rewarded her with rapid growth in the realm of retail business development.

Being of Portuguese and Italian descent, Jessica's heritage really shines through in all aspects of her personality. Raised in a house with 8 family members, dogs, cats, fish, reptiles, chickens, rabbits and birds all under one roof, she understands busy! Now she appreciates a smaller living space, surrounded by people and things that bring her joy - especially her partner and beloved animal companions. Jessica plans to develop her entrepreneurial spirit by working with small businesses to make big impacts on communities and continuing to publish her written work. She is determined to enrich her spiritual and personal growth and be a strong support system for her sisters and all the people she loves.

IG: @jessicadecastro

email: jessica.decastro@outlook.com

FB: Jessica De Castro

COURAGE

The courage that can appear within us even for a fraction of a moment can result in an undeniably beautiful transformation that can last a lifetime. In any given moment, we are only one decision away from leading an entirely different life. It is often the fear that is associated with the change, despite how badly the change is needed, that can counteract our efforts of becoming the greater version of ourselves we know exists within us. Courage is often confused with fearlessness, when it couldn't be farther from the truth. Courage is the driving force behind taking that leap, or making that choice despite the fear screaming loudly and our confidence dwindling with every moment that passes. Courage is a sense of deep, deep trust that even if it doesn't go according to plan, our momentary act of bravery got us one step closer.

Megan's story illustrates the life changing power of courage – the level of courage only those battling with the demons of addictions knows. Despite the odds of survival stacking against her every single moment that passes, Megan's story shows that even when we are faced with adversity, we can always choose higher for ourselves. It is never, ever too late.

HOPELESS DOPE FIEND TO DOPELESS HOPE FIEND

*"Every day I wake up, I get plugged into Spirit
and choose me."*

Megan Harmony

CHAPTER TWO

Hopeless Dope Fiend to Dopeless Hope Fiend

Statistically, I should be dead. I am filled with gratitude for the life I have and the fact I get to live it exactly as I want to; filled with hope, faith and courage. I do nothing out of obligation, or for the purpose of meeting anyone else's expectations. I live my life the way I live it because I want to, because I choose to, and because of my heart's satisfaction. It wasn't always this way.

March 3, 2010, the day I got sober, was the beginning of my becoming. It was a day like any other. I had come to after a night of partying. Guilt, shame and remorse came knocking and I was desperate for another way to live. On that morning, I was headed to a psych ward with little hope, feeling emotionally, mentally and spiritually bankrupt and as though the booze and drugs were my masters. They had me in their clutches and I felt as though this was how it was always going to be. I was so far off the beam of who I knew I was meant to be, and wasn't sure if it were even possible to achieve a life of anything greater. I was at a breaking point because to live was torture, but to die was terrifying. It was pure insanity as every day I found myself engaging in the same detrimental behaviours, yet expecting that I would somehow break free. My thoughts were clouded. I had tried everything imaginable to stop using substances; from not keeping any in the house, changing my phone number/getting a new phone with no contacts, spending time with family, avoiding everything social, switching from vodka to beer, dating a great guy, etc. You name it, I tried it. I had every reason humanly possible to not drink, and yet there I was on that brutally cold morning in March, hungover and spaced out from cocaine.

I had a great childhood. My parents separated when I was young but both of them loved me very much and provided amazing experiences for me. From a very young age I felt different though - being diagnosed with Diabetes at age four has that effect, but I didn't let that stop me. I soldiered on with the knowledge that I could die but wanting to enjoy every minute of life. My key phrase whenever something didn't go according to plan was "Oh well, can't worry about it!" and I lived by that as a young girl. I still remember it like it was yesterday. I had been teased again for getting a good mark on my grade 9 English exam. I was tired of being teased for being good so I thought that if I showed everyone how bad I could be the teasing would stop. I went to a friend's house that night to have a few drinks for the first time. I remember cracking the cap off the bottle of UFO, the cooler I had brought for the sole purpose of carrying out my plan. I remember the sound of it. I remember the smell of it. The taste was delicious and what I remember the most was the feeling. You know that feeling you get when you arrive home from work, sit down to relax and let out a sigh of relief? That's the feeling I'm talking about. In that moment, after that first sip, the world finally made sense. The voices inside my head that would constantly tell me that no one liked me subsided. I was able to talk to the boy that I had a crush on. I had a sense of confidence I had never experienced before. I had arrived. I proceeded to drink and smoke the night away. When I awoke the next morning, I saw that I had used my diabetic needle to carve the words "Life Sux" into my arm and my immediate thought was, "that was incredible I can't wait to do that again." Most people waking up to see a deliberate wound in their arm would never want to put themselves in that position again. Little did I know, in that moment I had crossed the invisible line into an 11 year battle with addictions.

Over the course of those years, my choice of substances increased in severity as I chased that feeling of freedom that the numbness would bring to me. I substituted beer for liquor, pot for ecstasy, and ecstasy for cocaine. I became addicted to more of whatever I could get my hands on including relationships, shopping, social media and work. I wasn't using daily, but I was using consistently. I would use anything and everything as a reason to get wasted. I got the guy, take some shots. It's sunny, snort some lines. Rainy, Netflix and beer. The boyfriend dumped me, wine with the girls. Simply being conscious was a reason to use. At the same time I was consistently making resolutions to quit. I never kept my promises. What I didn't realize is that I didn't have the power to, I had lost all control.

I remember one morning in particular with crystal clarity. I woke up to the sight of blood all over my pillow and it looked like a murder scene. I had snorted so much cocaine the night before that my nose bled out all night, long after I had passed out. What the hell is wrong with me? I was terrified. My mind was racing How did I end up like this? What am I doing with my life? What did the dealer cut it with? How am I going to fix this? I felt lost, broken, hopeless and worthless and again I found myself making the same resolution I had made so many times before: I'm never going to do this again. I locked myself in my bedroom for a week. I detoxed myself with the help of my partner (something I don't recommend to others without professional support). I went through agonizing pain, delirium tremens, and hallucinations, and all I wanted was to use again to be free of the torment in those moments. During that week of detoxing, to use meant to die, but to stop felt like death. It felt like a lose-lose situation.

Two months later we found out I was a month and a half pregnant. Divine intervention had protected my child from my addictions. I did not use throughout my pregnancy or while breastfeeding. It wasn't my willpower that kept me from using, because I knew I didn't have any. A Higher Power took the reins and ensured that this precious gift I had been given didn't suffer at my hands. On my own, I would have drank and used. Addiction is a subtle foe and even with every good and logical reason not to use, I would find a greater reason why I should, even if I didn't want to. That's the mental part of the spiritual malady, the obsession of the mind that takes hold in its death grip, and the only escape is to get drunk or high to shut up the insidious insanity. Even while pregnant, my addiction was still in charge, even when I thought it wasn't. What I did during my abstinence from cocaine and alcohol, was simply substitute it for other numbing obsessions like shopping, cleaning, gaming, social media and working so I was still very much at the beckoning of my addictions.

That was the longest I had gone without drinking or drugs in almost a decade and I would love to say that's where it ended. There I was, a new mother to a beautiful baby girl and the minute my daughter refused to breastfeed anymore I sent her to Grandma's and I went on a five-day drinking binge. My addict mentality told me I had earned it, and I believed it. I had this beautiful baby girl and I wanted more than anything to do right by her. None of my own thoughts even made any sense to me, so I can understand how atrocious my behaviour would have been to the outside world. Even more unfathomable is that the decision to use is made when sober and the moment it hits your system it triggers an insatiable desire for more. I would lose every ounce of power within me. My power to choose differently was immediately abolished the moment the substance entered my body. I could only choose more, and more would ultimately lead to more. I remember one night in particular. I dropped my daughter off at Grandma's with the bullshit promise of only having a couple of drinks. It was five days later that I finally came up for air. Five days. I was filled with guilt, shame and disgust with myself. I wanted to be a good mother. I wanted to be a healthy lover. I had dreams and aspirations, but as the fire raged on in my mind, so did the desperate need to numb. It was all part of the vicious cycle. I was like a locomotive carrying dynamite, with no conductor. I was out of control with no means to stop it.

Four years later, I found myself regaining consciousness in the intensive care unit, learning that my heart had stopped and I had been revived. Why did you try to kill yourself? The doctors were asking me. I had been on another bender and hadn't taken my insulin in ten days. I remember lying to them, trying to tell them that I loved my life and would never harm myself. The truth was, I was sick and tired of hurting everyone I loved and could see no other option than to drink myself to death, because I didn't have the guts to kill myself any other way. Not buying my story, I was admitted under the mental health act and my daughter celebrated her fourth birthday in her mother's hospital room. They kept telling me that alcohol was the problem, but in my mind it was the solution. They warned me that I would die within the year if I continued. That should have been enough to scare me back to health. I was discharged from the hospital on Christmas Eve with plans for a bright future with my daughter. Within five days, a friend stopped by to celebrate his promotion at work. We were going to have a glass of wine to celebrate - something within my addiction-controlled mind made me think this was safe. I woke up the next morning to all kinds of bottles in my kitchen and worse, this time my daughter had been home. The remorse and guilt were all over me, so I called my Mom to take her into her care, because at least then my child wouldn't be exposed to it. So she wouldn't be exposed to me, her own mother. By this point, I was not only incapable of caring for my own child, but I was also on a sick leave from work. My relationships were all strained as everyone I loved had walked away from me because they couldn't watch me self-destruct anymore. My addict-mind told me I had nothing left. Nothing to lose. I would go to my Mom's and put my daughter to sleep, and then I would go home and get drunk and snort cocaine. It was the only thing I knew of that would stop the self-hatred, and the feelings of complete hopelessness. One of those nights, my daughter, with tears in her beautiful blue eyes, looked at me and said "Mooma, please don't go tonight." I hugged her and said, "Don't worry honey, Mommy will be here when you wake up." In my mind, I wasn't lying. Anyone who says addicts are liars doesn't understand the nature of this disease. At that moment you could have put me on a lie detector and I would have passed with flying colours. I meant it when I told her I would be there in the morning. Three hours later, with tears pouring down my face, I walked out the door and so the spiral continued. Within weeks of that night, I was sent to a psychiatric hospital for major depression and severe anxiety, masked by severe alcoholism. I had taken a test with questions about how much alcohol and cocaine I consumed each day and I knew I had scored 200%. While there, that sweet voice of the young girl within me who used to say "Oh well, can't worry about it" said, "Go to the meeting."

When I walked through the door, the people were respectful and kind. A gentleman stuck out his hand, shook mine and said, "Welcome home, kid." While people were sharing their stories of addictions, for the first time ever, I didn't feel alone. These people thought like I thought. I didn't think they were being honest about staying sober though, as that seemed incredibly impossible to me at that time. But, I was so broken and done that I was willing to do whatever they suggested. Something had to change, so I dove into the step work. I grew to know myself, my shortcomings, my own higher power. I was able to stand fully in my truth and trust that God's got this. For the first time in my entire life, I took responsibility for what my life had become. I looked at everything that had happened through the lens of radical responsibility and I started to see how powerful taking ownership of my circumstances was. If I created this mess and it's no one else's fault, then no one else has to change for the damage to be repaired. I took my power back through connecting to a power greater than me as my source of strength, courage, security, abundance and love. Backed by this power, I was able to rectify the harms I had caused and let go of the victim mentality and past traumas I had clung to for far too long. The only person keeping me stuck was me. This revelation was a bit terrifying, because now I had to make the rest of my life the best of my life. It was the most freeing thought I had ever had. All I had to do was take the next right action and my life would be better than it was.

Six years into my sobriety, on a typical cold Canadian winter day in February, I received terrible news that a dear friend had passed away. I thought it was a cruel joke. I had just heard from him four days prior, and he said that his relapse was only a small one. He told me not to worry because he was returning to the meetings. He didn't make it there. I was shattered and I cried like I hadn't cried in years, and through the sobs I heard a voice say, "Don't let this death be in vain, this could have been you." I woke up to so many things that day. Although sober, I wasn't currently living a healthy life. I had gotten complacent, and wasn't who I wanted to be or who I knew I could be. On this day, as the news of my friend's passing sunk in, I realized that everything in life is temporary and merely on loan to us. I discovered that to have contented sobriety, the 12 steps must become an integral part of my everyday life. I can't stay sober on yesterday's soul-work. I had to embody them fully and wholeheartedly. I learned that old behaviours are not actually old if you are currently practicing them. Through my heartache, I made a decision, and that decision was to make my life count for something. I vowed to become the best version of myself I could possibly be.

I started to see the signs all around me reaffirming that I am meant to be here on earth. I started to believe that I have a story to tell, but knew I still had much work to do. I started doing inventories on the resentment, anger and fear that was holding me back. I started forgiving the people I was holding in my head and heart. I started practices to learn to love and forgive myself. I started talking to God again and it felt good, really good. I invested in myself, in my personal growth and I slowly started to feel a bit like me again. I walked away from any relationship that wasn't serving my highest good. I recognized that care for myself had to come first, before

I could care fully for another. Day by day I grew, until one day I realized I was no longer just hanging on and surviving. I was back in the driver's seat again. I was thriving.

Every day I wake up, I choose to stay connected to my Higher Power. I choose to see the good in humanity, look at the world through the lens of experience and all of the gifts I have been given. Every day I wake up, I get plugged into Spirit and choose me. March 3rd, 2019 marked nine years sober for me. Sobriety has allowed me to start my business, Soulful Sobriety, and share my experience with others. While I am incredibly proud of how far I have come, I know that the best is yet to come. I cannot wait to experience it. I revel in the present moment filled with hope, because I deserve an epic life and so do you!

"You can't go back and change the beginning, but you can start where you are and change the ending"

C.S. Lewis

Acknowledgements: Deepest thanks to my beautiful daughter, Trinity, my greatest spiritual teacher, who reminds me to stay in the present and be in wonder of it all. I'd also like to acknowledge the 12-step fellowships, for being there when I was ready to stop, for good and for all.

About the Author

Megan Harmony is steadfast in her dedication to living a life based in love. She is kind-hearted and compassionate in nature, and offers a safe place to land. She has an old-soul with a young spirit, and is a gorgeous example of Soul-Full living. Having overcome many adverse circumstances, she is a champion at rising up and rebuilding when all seemed lost. She has made it her mission to help others live life to the fullest. She also advocates that IT IS possible to recover from alcoholism and addictions, because she herself has overcome them and is living life on purpose!

Megan is always full of life and wonderment, her connection to Spirit makes her a radiant beam of light that can't help but call you in. Megan is courageous and faces challenges with a brave heart. She is an eternal optimist and many say she is irreplaceable, unforgettable and their lives have forever changed through her presence. Her lived experience, as well as her practical nurse diploma, addictions care-worker diploma, and master-level Arcturian Reiki practitioner, make her uniquely qualified to assist people through their most difficult times.

Megan founded her business, Soulful Sobriety, in 2019 in which she is a soul coach, inspirational speaker, author and Reiki healer. She helps people thrive through adversity and stay sober through it all. She teaches how to live life loving yourself, feeling worthy and excited for each new day. In her spare time, Megan can be found spending time with her family-specifically her daughter, who is her greatest blessing, reading, painting, singing or planning the next big adventure.

IG: @soulful_sobriety

FB: @SoulfulSobriety

STRENGTH

Strength is what allows us to trust ourselves to navigate the darkness, as we trip and fumble our way towards the light. It gives us the will to take another step, breathe another breath and pick ourselves up as many times as we need to. Strength keeps us alive, when it becomes almost impossible to understand why we should go on another day, when we are living with a monstrous amount of pain in our hearts.

Shannon's story gives hope and courage to all, that it is possible to navigate the tsunami of grief and everything it leaves in its wake. That even when we don't identify with what it means to be strong, that we must trust that we are; that even in our weakest moments, strength still has a home within us. Strength is what pushes us to do even the simplest of things like getting out of bed, eating some food, and taking ourselves for a walk. It is what fights for us to do what we need to do to keep our own hearts beating. Strength gives us permission to live.

BYE BABY, I LOVE YOU

"There are times, that the outside world will never see, when you must be braver than brave and stronger than strong in order to survive."

–Shannon Miller

CHAPTER THREE

Bye Baby, I Love You

The buzz of my phone brought me back to reality. What had I been thinking about and why was my phone buzzing? Buzz. Buzz. Confused and disoriented, I realized that someone was texting me. Where was my phone? Where am I? I felt strangely lost in a place that should have felt safe and familiar. There it is. The kitchen table. Yes, that's right, I'm in the kitchen. My legs ached as I willed them to move the impossibly long distance toward my phone. How long had I been standing there? I reached my phone and saw that it was a text from my sister, Sandy. It read, 'Hi Shan. How are you doing?' I began to shake. Everything that I had been attempting to bury deep inside of me, the sadness, the fear, the pain, and the never-ending yearning for my Kaiti, all rushed to the surface. I wasn't okay. I'm not okay. As the tsunami of grief washed over me, my thumbs fumbled around as I struggled to text back, 'not good'. Seconds later my phone rang. It was Sandy. I answered with a whisper of a hello, barely able to speak and with no strength left within me to hold it in any longer. 'Oh Shan...' Sandy said. I could feel the mountainous wave tossing my insides around as it made its way from the depths of my core to the lips of my mouth as it fought its way to escape. I began to cry. My crying turned to sobbing, my sobbing turned to wailing. It was a wail from the deepest part of my being that could only portray pain; deep, unrelenting, unforgiving emotional pain. I gasped for air as each painful wave of despair washed over me. I couldn't speak. The only sounds I could make were painful moans, bone chilling cries and primal screams. Endless tears fell from my eyes as the tsunami of pain struggled to be released. My legs grew weaker as I was being drowned by my own grief. Slowly, I sank to the floor. Like an old time movie, the memories and events of the last few weeks played out raw and jagged in my mind. It was like having a front row seat to a horror movie at the theatre. Only, this wasn't a movie and it wasn't a nightmare because there would be no waking up from this terror and going back to my happy life. This was my reality.

'Bye baby, I love you'.

'Bye mamma, I love you too'.

The last words my baby girl ever said to me...the last words I ever said to my baby girl.

CO

The sun was beginning to rise, and I was admiring its radiant colours as I drove to work. Blazing red and orange, glowing yellow, vibrant purple and pink. So beautiful. April 15, 2014. As the song finished playing on the radio, a news report came on. The reporter's voice was low and pained as he spoke of a mass murder at a house party in the early morning. I couldn't breathe, my chest ached as I clenched my steering wheel with all my strength. It can't be! Panic surged through me and I could hear my blood gushing through my veins. Stop it! I yelled to myself. Don't think such horrible things! My mind drifted to our last phone call barely two days prior. I could hear the happiness in Kaiti's voice as she told me that she was going to a house party the next night. I was so excited for her because she was a homebody and very rarely went to parties. How could I have encouraged her to go?!?! Kaiti's spirits were light and carefree as she chatted on about her upcoming week and all the plans she had for her future. She was happy. My beautiful, intelligent, funny, caring and incredibly talented daughter was happy and my heart was full.

My heart was shattering into a million little pieces. As tears fell from my eyes, I struggled to carry on to work. My dashboard clock glowed green. 7:00 am. My mind was racing. Kaiti would still be asleep. Okay, I told myself, I'll wait until 8:30am to call her. I attempted to put my crazy thoughts to rest. Kaiti is fine. My baby is fine. The horror movie continues... there is no way for me to stop it. My life, as I knew it, was ending. I spent the next hour sitting rigidly at my desk, doing no work, only staring at the clock on my computer. Tick. Tick. Tick. 8:30am never came. At 8:21am my eyes were jolted away from my computer clock by the sound of my phone ringing. My heart sank and the tears came again as I reached for my phone. Please, please, no. It was my ex-husband. 'Come to my house. Something has happened to Kaiti'.

I arrived, so afraid and with a terrible sinking feeling in my gut. I remember standing on the sidewalk as I saw my son crossing the street towards me. He looked con-fused and afraid too as we both desperately searched for an explanation for this meeting. He asked, 'Is it Grandpa?' I began to shake my head no, when I caught a glimpse of my children's father coming out of his house. He was walking towards us, and his pace quick-ened and turned into a run. He was running towards us, his face grimacing with a pain like I had never seen on him before. That's when I saw them – two detectives standing on the sidewalk. I started to step backwards. I didn't want to hear it. No, no, no! As he reached us, he pulled us both close to him. I can remember resisting his embrace; I pushed hard against his chest. Panic and dread were surfacing as I fought in disbelief. "Kaiti's been murdered." he choked out. Not my Kaiti! Not my baby! I struggled to break free, to run away from the despair of my ex-husband's embrace. I wanted to es-cape the shocking truth. My Kaiti was gone.

Looking back, I can honestly say that I don't know how I survived. I had to do things that no mother should ever have to endure. Seeing the look in my oldest daughter's eyes as she screamed out in pain, "She was my person; Kaiti is my person!" as I ran to her after the news broke. Holding my son's hand during the trial while his whole body shook in anger as we sat through the details of that horrific night. Sliding my hand off of the coffin after saying good-bye to Kaiti as she was wheeled away to be cremated. These are things that no mother should ever have to endure. As unbearable as all of those events were, and there were many others I haven't mentioned, there was one single event that almost broke me. In fact, I've never shared this with anyone. It has taken me years to even share it with myself for I've had to put the memory in the deepest depths of my soul in order to survive. No mother, no parent should ever come to know the pain of identifying their child's body.

The weather turned cold the day after Kaiti died and I remember shivering as we drove to the Coroner's office. I knew, in my soul, that I wasn't shivering from the cold, but from fear and shock. When we arrived, we were guided towards a door. I started to see black spots, my mind was spinning. Breathe, just breathe. My heart was pounding painfully loud and I whispered to myself over and over again, My baby, my Kaiti. My baby, my Kaiti. As I stepped through the door of the viewing room, my eyes instantly found the monitor. "NO!" I screamed from the darkest depths of my soul. With no strength left in me, I collapsed to the floor. But I NEEDED to see her! I NEEDED to tell her I loved her. I NEEDED to comfort and soothe her. Crawling closer and closer to the video screen that showed my beautiful child, memories started to flash through my mind as I stared at her breathless face. Pictures of me pregnant with Kaiti, rubbing my swollen belly as I whispered to her all my hopes and dreams of her future and how I would protect her from harm; Kaiti just after her birth with a thick patch of black, black hair; Kaiti as a toddler taking a huge bite out of a chocolate Easter bunny with her now blonde hair falling over her eyes; Kaiti dancing ever so gracefully on stage; Nicky and Kaiti laughing and singing at the top of their lungs as we drove to the family cottage in the summer while their brother Josh sat in his car seat smiling. SLAM! My brain snapped back to the present moment and there, in front of me, was my reality on the video screen. My heart breaks as I realize that this image on the screen is now a memory that will forever be part of all the beautiful ones.

In the days following, I struggled to function. My senses were heightened. The dimmest of lights were so blindingly bright.   The soft whispers of conversation were deafeningly loud. People were everywhere, yet I felt so very, very alone. I was flooded with kindness as so many people just wanted to help. So much compassion, so much love, so much caring. Yet none of it would bring my Kaiti back to life. And the world continued on....

That is not the end of my story. My story continues, because now the healing has begun and it began on one particular morning in October 2014. I awoke feeling completely broken. Shattered. I lay in bed knowing that I couldn't go on this way and that I had a decision to make. Do I want to give in and fall deeper into this dark pit of grief? Or do I want to try to live a happy life once again? I knew that either option would be one of the hardest things I have ever done. That morning, I chose happiness and I allowed myself to think about what it would take to achieve it. One thing I knew for certain was that I would need to heal not only my body and my mind but most importantly, my soul.

I began with what I knew. I knew how to heal my body. Shock, trauma, stress, sleepless nights and indescribable heartbreak had left my body and mind barely functioning. I had very little physical or emotional strength, so I took baby steps. I started eating healthy, I walked a little bit each day, and I started looking for joy in the little things and as difficult as it was, I started to feel gratitude for the 23 years that I had the gift of being Kaiti's mamma and it began to supersede the overwhelming sense of devastation that she was no longer with me. Sometimes there are still days where the best I can do is breathe, and I have gratitude for that. Gratitude is where the healing of my soul is being done. For me, having gratitude, especially for the little things, is what has gotten me through the hardest times. Sunshine warming my face. A telephone call from one of my kids. Kaiti's cat purring next to me. My dog Gracie's head on my lap, when I'm having a sad day. A text from a friend. Hearing a song on the radio that Kaiti did a dance routine to. Playing board games with my family. A gentle yoga routine. Holding my grandbaby as he sleeps. These are the things that warm my soul.

I have been blessed to have caring, compassionate and supportive people in my life. These people have stayed by my side in my darkest of times and now are by my side, encouraging me as I move forward as I strive to live my life with passion and purpose. Because so many wonderful people were there for me, I now strive to be there for others who have experienced similar trauma or loss. Some people need to yell and scream, some people need someone to sit with them so they are not alone, and other people need to tell stories and share memories. Some need a hand to help pull them out of their dark pit, some need to know I understand, and others just need to cry and know it's okay to do so.

I have been asked more than once, "How did you survive?" To some, my answer may sound too easy, when in reality it isn't. My answer is, I chose to survive. I have to remind myself each and every day that I have a choice to continue on, and take steps towards my continued healing. Every single day I must remind myself.

Breathe. Wrap your precious memories of Kaiti with love and place them gently in your heart. Spend time with family. Rest. Do the best you can, whatever that may look like. Be kind to yourself. Let others help you; you don't have to do this alone. Cry. Seek out a strong and caring community. Laugh. Let go of the guilt and the anger. Find a purpose. Move your body. Do whatever it takes to climb out of the darkness. Love. Speak your truth. Stand in the sunshine. Do what warms your soul.

Most importantly, I have to give myself permission to feel all the feelings. Once I was able to give myself permission to feel the sadness, the fear, the pain and longing, I was able to give myself permission to feel the love, the joy, the light, and the hope for the future. The word Saudade describes the feeling in my heart. It depicts how a person's absence can be felt in a quarreling combination of happiness and sadness. I am filled with sadness because I miss my Kaiti and I can feel her absence every day, in every breath I take, while at the same time I am filled with happiness that I have so many beautiful memories of her to hold in my heart for the rest of my life.

I truly believe that I died the day Kaiti died and I have since come back as a different person. I am learning to live this new life with a piece of my heart and soul forever missing. I had no control over what happened to Kaiti, but each day I wake up to the same choice. Most days I choose to live a happy, peaceful, healthy life. A life that is filled with love and light, sunshine and laughter, memories and tears, and hope with the birth of my grandson. Other days the best I can choose to do is to keep breathing, and that is good, too. Healing does not just happen. Time does not heal all wounds. One does not just simply 'get over it' or 'move on'. Healing takes effort. Healing takes commitment. Healing takes energy. Healing takes love. Healing takes forgiveness of oneself. Healing takes a lifetime. I will forever miss my Kaiti, but I know she is with me always. I carry her love with me everywhere I go.

Acknowledgements: For all who are shattered after the death of a loved one, may my story bring you hope. My heartfelt thanks for all the love, support and encouragement I received in writing this chapter from both my family – Kaiti, whose presence I felt throughout this beautiful process, Nicky, Josh and Loris; and from Sarah Swain, whose guidance and belief in me and my story meant everything to me.

About the Author

Shannon Miller is the proud mamma of three amazing children - Nicky, Kaiti, and Josh. She is a traumatic grief survivor. Her world was completely shattered when her daughter, Kaiti, was brutally murdered in 2014. After realizing six months later that she had a choice to either stay in the depths of her darkness and grief OR live this new life with purpose and joy, Shannon chose to LIVE! She honoured her grief and allowed herself to feel all the feelings that come with the pain and sorrow, and then began taking steps towards healing. Shannon is now a grief guide, where she coaches people as they walk through the darkness of their grief and learn to live life after loss.

Shannon is an inspirational speaker and is featured on the "The Great Canadian Woman" podcast, where she shares her story of life after the death of her daughter with others, so that they know they are not alone and that they CAN survive and live a full and happy life in spite of their grief, fear, and loss. She has also been invited multiple times to be a guest speaker at a university justice class sharing the point of view from a victim's perspective. Shannon is an active member of the Calgary Homicide Support Society and is a trauma support advocate to families of murdered loved ones. As a passionate believer in having real and raw conversations about all things surrounding grief, Shannon has created a Facebook page called "Conversations with Shannon" where she openly discusses her life and the lessons she has learnt since the death of Kaiti.

https://conversationswithshannon.com

IG @conversations_with_shannon

FB @conversationswithshannon

DISCERNMENT

To discern is to have an ability to detect the difference in what appears to lie in front of us versus what it actually means. To discern requires the courage to reject what we see at the surface, knowing that there is more to it than this. It is the desire to peel back the layers with a sense of curiosity, and read between the lines when we know in our gut there is a deeper reason, meaning or solution.

Sue's story illustrates the importance of knowing ourselves beneath our own surface. It is a story of a woman who ran from her painful adolescence, only to find the pain still embedded deep inside her as she moved into adulthood. A beautiful journey of self-awareness, and the uniqueness of every body. It encourages us to go deep within our cells to find the true source of our pain, because our answers always come from within.

WHAT HOLDS US, MOLDS US

"We all have the power to heal our cells."

–Susan Ruhe

CHAPTER FOUR

What Holds Us,

Molds Us

"The cure for pain is in the pain." - Rumi

Uniqueness lies within all of us. We all hold unique stories deep within our bodies. Everything we've experienced, endured, suffered through and felt throughout our lives stays with us, embedded in our cells. All that we are in this very moment is a direct accumulation of every event, good or bad, that we have experienced, like a cellular road map of our journey. We can choose to remain stuck in the paths that have been ingrained within us, or we can change the course. This is our power. I didn't fully understand this concept until I began tapping into human fascia. When I began my career in Massage Therapy, I focused my practice around a technique called Myofascial Release Therapy (MFR) within the first year, because it absolutely changed the game for me and my clients. You see, human fascia is every-thing. Literally. Our movements, our injuries, our surger-ies, our thoughts, our feelings, our experiences, our entire being, is encapsulated in fascia. Our fascial sys-tem connects every single cell in our body, like the glue that holds us together. "Fascia is very densely woven, covering and interpenetrating every muscle, bone, nerve, artery and vein, as well as all of our internal or-gans including the heart, lungs, brain and spinal cord. It is one continuous structure that exists from head to toe without interruption."[1] Fascia is very protective. It holds us tighter in areas of trauma, injury and postural imbal-ance, which means it also engulfs our memories, feel-ings and experiences, all within its cellular wrapping.

MFR is so powerful because over time these tightened areas begin to create blockages within the body, kind of like cement. These cement-like areas start to cause pain elsewhere in the body as it tries to compensate. MFR helps to shift, change, and expand those areas, increas-ing flow and decreasing pain wherever that may be showing up. MFR encourages alignment within the body, and an aligned body is a happy body! This all be-came true for me when I began practicing this tech-nique and analyzing my own battle with anxiety, stress, headaches and body pain.

From what I can recall, the pain began to creep in dur-ing my teenage years. I think we can agree that high school was a trivial time for many, and I can remember

---

[1] https://www.myofascialrelease.com/about/fascia-definition.aspx

walking through those halls wishing I was invisible. With my head pounding, blood boiling, and my stomach tied up in knots, the nervousness would consume me each and every day. In the eleventh grade, I found myself stealing acetaminophen from the medicine cabinet every morning before heading out the door, just to numb myself out. That year was a total blur. Not only was I silently self-medicating, but I started seeking other alternatives to try to cover it up. Alcohol, marijuana, sex, food, whatever I could get my hands on. These were things that would help me hide, by masking what I was really feeling and altering my perception of what was really going on inside.

The truth is, pain in the body is very difficult to measure because most of the time we can't see it. Pain is something that we each feel differently and for most of us, it's difficult to explain to others. For me, the pain was invisible, making it nearly impossible to articulate during that time of my life.

So what was actually causing all of this stress in my body? Why was I consumed with aches and pains, physically, mentally and emotionally? When I reflect upon my childhood, nothing out of the ordinary stands out. I had a great home, good parents, an abundance of opportunities before me. But I can remember feeling very alone throughout all of it, spending the majority of my time crying in my room, completely consumed with thoughts of unworthiness and fear. Maybe I felt ashamed? Maybe I didn't know what was going on and it was just easier to keep quiet. I understand now that there's only so much we can hold onto before the heaviness causes us to crumble.

Following high school, I ran from my hometown to start a new life. I thought that if I could escape the energy I had grown up surrounding myself in, I would become who I wanted to be and feel good within my own skin. I hadn't yet drawn the connection that my healing needed to come from within, and I quickly realized that physically leaving where my most anxious memories existed wasn't the sole solution. It wasn't the only answer and as a surprise to me then, things only got worse. I felt even more alone, more anxious, with more headaches and back pain, all in a new city where I knew a total of three people. The stress had built up like bricks and I felt like I was suffocating. Panic attacks, insomnia, migraines and weight gain were now the heaviest of my burdens and nothing within my body felt real anymore. I was sinking as depression steered the ship. I couldn't sleep, but I also couldn't get out of bed. I couldn't eat, but oddly enough I could drink and smoke all day long. I was crashing and desperately needed help.

One cloudy afternoon in May of 2005, I stepped through the doors of the Women's Health Clinic for the first time. I remember feeling heavily guarded at first, since I hadn't seen a doctor in years, but I instantly felt welcome. After a lengthy conversation with the doctor surrounding my health history, and several tests later, she gave me two options. She could prescribe me antidepressants, which she was hesitant to do based on my age, or I could commit to start healing my body from the inside out. That was probably the first time in my life that I had felt any hope in feeling good within my body. Also, it was the first time I had ever worked with a female doctor. Coincidence? Not sure. But I knew deep down that I didn't want to take any medications, and I was determined to find a natural solution that could help propel my health in the right direction. I figured, what did I have to lose, besides the pain?

Nothing happened overnight. I started small — water, vitamins, yoga, and massage treatments, to name a few. I gave up sugar, alcohol and large double-doubles. But, it didn't take long for my body to start improving. I could sleep again. My headaches were lessening. I stopped gaining weight. I had energy to work. These simple improvements were making a huge difference! How did I live for so long without knowing the impact of such simple habits on my body?

A few months into my career, I continued to struggle with mild anxiety. My body pain had diminished, but I could still feel that something was stuck. A colleague and I began practicing the art of MFR together, by working on each other regularly, and that's where the big ah-ha moments started to happen. This is where she worked in my abdomen for the first time. This is where all the pieces of the puzzle fell into place. As I was lying on the table, her fingers pressing in and around my navel, old thoughts, old feelings and old emotions started flooding into my mind like a tidal wave. My body began to shake, uncontrollably. Tears ran down my face. All of the shit I had buried from my past began resurfacing in my mind. What was happening to me? Her fingers burned as she slowly glided through my abdomen. The energy exchange was like nothing we had experienced before. It was magic!

When she stopped and I stood up, I could feel that my body had changed. Things had shifted within me, on a cellular level. I felt lighter, I felt taller, I could breathe bigger, and my back pain was different. She had found the source. This experience remains to be one of the most pivotal events of my life. It not only transformed the way I felt within my body, but it also changed the path of my career.

Over the past ten years I've been diving deep into women's abdominal fascia, tapping into the anxiety, emotions and pain that swirl around in there. It's crazy how much we hold. For instance, do you ever catch yourself clenching your stomach for no particular reason? Then, when you realize it's happening, you just let it go, allowing your abdomen to relax and your shoulders to fall. This habitual holding pattern within my body was, without a doubt, the root cause of my pain. Holding it in and blocking my flow. This is not how our bodies want to work.

Let's all just take a moment to let it go, shall we? Let's all take a DEEP BREATH together. Ready?

Inhale. Expand your abdomen and chest, push your navel out. Create enormous space within your abdomen and slowly allow your lungs to fill up.

Now softly exhale.

Beautiful.

Let's do that one more time.

Inhale (1,2,3,4)

Exhale (1,2,3,4)

Perfect.

This has always been my struggle, and that of so many other women with whom I've worked. Enormous stress, anxiety and pain originates from our core. By tapping into abdominal fascia, expanding it within myself and helping clients do the same, it is evident that we all share this similar experience. We all hold it in, whether we realize it or not. In this pattern, I catch myself innately squeezing my stomach while I'm working, doing the dishes or the laundry, driving, everywhere, all the time. Even on the days when I feel really, really good, it just happens. This is how my fascia has held me, creating significant restrictions throughout my body, constantly blocking the flow, altering my posture and producing physical and emotional pain. I can now reflect on how I felt walking through those cold high school halls, realizing that this pattern of holding on, sucking in and not breathing fully, only amplified during that time in my life. It's a pattern that remains as I focus to reverse daily.

With every MFR treatment, given or received, a lot of magic can happen on the massage table. Accessing restricted areas we've held onto for so long can cause our bodies to shake, cry, tremble, whatever the body needs to do to allow it to shift. Some people experience visions of their past lives, which still blows my mind. Some see colours and auras as their treatments evolve. Some cry and convulse uncontrollably, and it's all okay. We need to embrace these cellular shifts and breathe into them, so we can heal our wounds and move past them. Our pain, our trauma, our anxiousness will never fully leave our bodies, but we can push beyond it, allowing us to feel all the new and wonderful experiences that await us.

I often wonder how many others are struggling with this right now. How many are hiding their physical and emotional pain and silently suffering? In 2016, 3,926 Canadians ended their lives due to suicide, according to the Canadian Association for Suicide Prevention. I truly believe that I could have been a part of this statistic if I hadn't followed the path I did. There were some very dark days.

I wish I had learned more about my body earlier on in my life. I wish I had known how important physical alignment was to our overall health and well-being. I wish I had known how powerful fascia was before becoming a therapist. But maybe I just needed to feel as if I was dying before I could feel alive again. Maybe everything happened for a reason, and I was meant to heal first so I could in turn help others. Within every healing experience, I have discovered that in order for us to shift or push past all that is holding us back, keeping us stuck, is the simple fact that we have to feel it. We have to lean into our pain, acknowledge it, breathe into it, to truly overcome it. If we simply ignore it, the long-term effects are insurmountable.

As we travel along our individual paths, it is important to know that we all have the ability to choose. We can choose to remain stuck in our pain and continue to self-medicate, masking all that is hindering us, or we can figure out what our cells truly need to feel good. We can choose to face and embrace all that is uncomfortable within ourselves in order to heal. The past cannot be changed. It will always exist in our bodies, but our future, well, we always have more control over that.

My mission is to help guide the next generation, because I wish I had someone guiding me with the knowledge that I have now. For some reason, the importance of learning about our cells has gotten lost, while the majority are simply searching for a quick fix. We are made up of the exact same material. Doesn't it make the most sense to understand it as much as we can? The only difference lies within our individual experiences from the moment we take our first breath. We can't change our past, but we can always work on healing, learning and navigating our bodies into the future.

It is important to know that we're not alone when it comes to the struggles we face within our bodies. And we are lucky enough to live in a time where self-care is cool and we can share our stories, our challenges, and our triumphs on social media and with our girl gang without guilt or fear. If I could offer one piece of advice, it would be this: I want you to, without question, wholeheartedly love your cells. Love them so hard, that you will stop at nothing to make them happy. After all, every body is a puzzle and it's up to us to find the pieces that may be missing, within our cells, for us to feel whole again. If I can do this and if my clients can do this, so can you.

"Take care of your body. It's the only place you have to live."
–Jim Rohn

Acknowledgement: Thank you to my gorgeous girl, Avalina. You are my greatest gift and the reason I continue to strive higher in this life.

About the Author

 Susan Ruhe B.A., R.M.T., is a mother, massage therapist, writer and educator. For over a decade, Susan has practiced the art of Myofascial Release Therapy (MFR) through which she helps her clients to align their bodies and eliminate pain. She believes that by identifying the root cause of pain and discomfort, we can naturally heal our bodies both physically and emotionally, as it is all connected. Throughout her career she has discovered that working with teenagers and young adults provides the greatest impact with regards to preventative healthcare. She firmly believes that we all deserve to live in peace within our bodies, and helping to educate and guide our youth has become her mission.

Growing up in Welland, Ontario, Sue dedicated most of her extracurricular time to competitive highland dancing, giving her the opportunity to perform at both Disneyland and Disney World before the age of 14. This skill and these experiences helped propel her towards her greatest passions - the human body and travelling! When she left her hometown to attend Western University followed by the D'Arcy Lane Institute for massage therapy, London, Ontario became her new home. She has since built a reputable client base, started a family, and remains dedicated to empowering the youth in her community. With travelling being her second passion, you can find her and her family nestled in the sand, toes in the ocean, soaking up the Caribbean sun, every chance they can get.

We must enjoy what we love and feel good doing it!

Website: www.loveyourcells.ca

COMPASSION

Compassion is the way in which we show empathy for the one who feels pain, even when that pain lashes out towards us. It is our ability to see the human hidden beneath all of the sadness and suffering, and the heart behind all of the hurt. Compassion is our sense of knowing and understanding that the painful and sometimes shocking behaviour we witness in others, has a thread that traces back to a deep, deep wound that never fully healed.

Falon's story not only speaks to the importance of having compassion for others as they navigate their own journey, but the need to have compassion for ourselves as we care for our own hearts in the process. It's a story of love, loss and the confusing and difficult territory of Post-Traumatic Stress Disorder.

LEST WE FORGET

"Love First"

Falon Joy Malec

CHAPTER FIVE

Lest We Forget

People come into our lives for a reason. They come to teach us lessons and guide us down new paths along life's journey. They arrive in time to support you through tough times and encourage you to achieve your goals. I have been fortunate to have many great mentors, friends and loved ones in my life to do just that. After an unhealthy, abusive relationship, I spent a great deal of time trying to get ahead financially and in doing so, lost sight of what was most important. I became terrified of being broke and developed an obsession for making money. I had spent a few years bouncing around from province to province, from job to job, brokerage to brokerage, and apartment to apartment before finally, the universe stepped in and shattered my world around me.

I had dated on and off for a few years after leaving my fiancé. Most were frivolous and empty affairs whom I met online with the ease of swiping right. I used them to convince myself I held value and worth, something I lost during the six-year relationship prior. But the universe has a way of stepping in and making course corrections when you become too blind to make them yourself. Meeting Kurtis was that intervention. It wasn't planned, I wasn't looking and I tried to avoid it. We met around the end of February to early March of 2014 when the Canadian Military Services called Veteran Affairs (VA) had stopped sending him support payments he was due after his injuries sustained in Afghanistan. He'd lost a leg four years prior while on patrol as a Combat Engineer (1 CER, Task Force 3-09) and had been receiving benefits from VA which he was currently fighting to retain. When they stopped sending his cheques, he wasn't able to pay many of his bills, his insurance policies being among them. After he'd explained his situation, as his broker, I did whatever I could to find him a solution and keep his policies in force until he could pay the bills. Without his car, he wouldn't be able to take his daughter to school or spend the day with his son before picking up his daughter again in the afternoon. He was so appreciative of my help that he insisted I allow him to take me for a drink as a thank you. I tried to refuse, given he was my client, but something inside told me I needed to go. I'm so grateful that I did.

Kurtis came into my life at a time when I was still healing from a broken heart and showed me what a good man could be. He was there when I needed him, he treated me with respect and did thoughtful things to make my days better and brighter. He made me feel valued and worth loving. He showed me that men can be good fathers to their children and be dedicated to making sure they are loved and looked after. He showed me that husbands and wives can be best friends after divorce, as we often spent time together as one big family.

Kurtis also showed me what Post-Traumatic Stress Disorder (PTSD) can look like, something which I'd had zero experience with, or understanding of, like the majority of Canadians. He fought against his demons for a long time, mostly in silence with very little complaint. But, no matter his strength and resilience, occasionally those demons took over and sent him into a pit of despair and darkness that our veterans know all too well. The first time it happened, I didn't know what it was and barely caught a glimpse. He occasionally used street drugs to cope. I was accustomed to dating men who used drugs and thought nothing of the visit from his dealer and went to bed alone that night, leaving him upstairs with his poisons.

I left for work that morning, with Kurtis asleep on the couch. It would be three days before I heard from him while he did what his demons commanded. He shut me out in an attempt to keep me from seeing the destruction. It would be several months before it happened again, only this time it was much worse and I saw it all. I saw the agony and torture in his eyes. I saw the darkness that lurked underneath, eating away at his spirit. I saw the drinking. I saw the drugs. I saw the recklessness and intentional self-destruction. And I was terrified. I was confused. But worst of all, I misunderstood what I saw. Blinded by my own brokenness, I couldn't see that his behaviour was that of someone who desperately needed help, love and support, and a safe place to land. Instead, what I saw was a repeat experience of bad ex-boyfriends. I saw a man using me for a place to drink and do drugs. I ended our relationship harshly after he left my home in a bad state of liquor bottles and cigarette packages.

Several months would pass before we spoke again. He had reached out and apologized for what happened. While spending some time together he explained a little more about what was going on and how he sometimes lost control of himself and did things he knew he shouldn't. He just couldn't seem to say "no". We made plans to help him learn to run with his prosthetic leg, and spent a few months together walking trails in the river valley to exercise and test it out. We barbecued with his mom and the kids, and I started to believe I should let him back in. Although I didn't fully understand, I felt in my heart that I needed to be there for him. I wanted to be there. But I was still afraid. Afraid of what he was dealing with. Afraid of how much he meant to me. Afraid of getting too close and having my heart broken. And sure enough, before I could even decide for myself, he shut me out again. Instead of fighting for him and being there the way he needed, I let him leave. I was hurt. I was angry and frustrated because I just couldn't understand.

More months passed as I threw myself back into my work and spent most of my days at the office working 12-16 hours. I shut people out and put making money back as a top priority. New romances failed and friendships began to suffer, but I told myself I had to work hard if I was going to achieve the things I wanted. Kurtis did eventually reach out again, and I did meet with him a few times for a meal or a walk. But this time I had closed myself off a little bit more. I wouldn't risk being hurt again.

The following summer, while watching Country Strong with my mom, Garret Hedlund started singing "Give into me", to Leighton Meester, and like a tsunami, knocking the very breath out of my chest, I realized that I was in love with him. Deeply. And I was horrified. Terrified. I fought back tears and failed. As the tears slid down my cheeks I wondered how the hell that had happened. And even more importantly, how the hell was I supposed to deal with it? Kurtis didn't care what anyone thought of him, what he did or what he believed. And that's why I loved him. From his beautiful, soul touching eyes to the "Jesus hates a Pussy" tattoo on his wrist, I loved all of him because he was real and authentic. He wore his heart on his sleeve. What you saw was what you got. I sat on this newfound knowledge for months mulling over whether or not I should tell him. Guilt is a heavy burden when you lose someone. And Mortality Motivation is a very real thing.

On December 15, 2015 while sitting at my desk at the office trying to catch up on work, Kurtis invited me to join him and the family for dinner. I declined the invitation. I had just spent three days out of the office buying a new car and was desperately trying to catch up before heading to Ontario for an early Christmas trip. I told him I was too busy and asked for a rain check as I was flying out the next afternoon and still needed to pack. As always, he understood and agreed to wait until the new year.

On December 18, 2015 at 7:51 am, I woke up like any other morning and checked my messages. Seven hours prior, Kurtis had sent me a few texts. The first message said that the previous week had been tough on him. Had I not silenced my phone I would have heard his ringtone and been able to respond. I often wonder if things may have turned out differently if I had. At 3:36 am he sent another text, which, among other things said, "you're a good person and are going to succeed past your expectations".

I knew in my gut that something was wrong and messaged him right away. Receiving no reply, I called his phone. No answer. By 8:53 am, while standing over my mom's kitchen sink, coffee cup gripped in shaking hands, his mom called. My heart sank to the pit of my stomach like a lead weight. I crumpled into a heap on the floor, as she told me the news I knew all morning was coming.

Kurtis, amongst many wonderful and beautiful things, was also a painful life lesson and a reminder of what is most important. Through all his hardships he stayed true to his friends and loved ones. They always came first, no matter what he was struggling with. And struggle he did. He was a reminder to love first. To spend time with those who matter and to be vulnerable enough to tell them how much you love and value them. My mind felt flooded with how I could have handled our relationship differently. I wasn't aware or understanding enough of his struggles with PTSD, and assumed his behaviours were those of a selfish, self-centered person, when in reality, they were the symptoms of a disease he struggled with daily in silence. Through my own fears and self-preservation, I held back my true feelings and never shared with him how much he actually meant to me and just how much I loved him. I had convinced my-self that it was better for him that he not know, because knowing could throw him off course as he fought to im-prove his life, when in reality, I was just afraid he didn't feel the same. And so he died, never knowing.

Instead of joining him for dinner in the New Year, I was attending his wake at the funeral home. Somehow, alt-hough the funeral home was packed with friends, family and brothers in service, I was blessed with a few mo-ments alone with him. I told him everything I never said and kissed him goodbye for the last time, tucking a let-ter filled with apologies and memories under his peace-fully folded hands. Joining everyone at the Legion afterwards was difficult and painful. My time with Kurt was intimate and shared only with his immediate family and occasionally his best friend, Lyndon. Surrounded by a sea of strangers, I clung to his mom as though she was a life raft. I was overwhelmed and felt like a fraud. I didn't belong there. I had no right to be there celebrat-ing his life when I hadn't been there enough to support him when he was alive. And so, I left early, overwhelmed with grief and guilt. I went home where I spent the bet-ter part of a year hating myself, struggling with my thoughts and begging the universe to strike me down with anything that would end my life so I could see him again and tell him how sorry I was.

While I now realize that things happened as they were always meant to happen, Kurt's death has changed me forever. He brought many incredible people into my life, people I now consider to be family. Some I met while he was alive, some came afterwards during a toboggan party with the kids and a Nerf dart to the butt. He brought us all together to make sure the people he loved most would be looked after in his absence. He knew it would take a village to do what he did so effortlessly.

After his funeral, I returned to work refusing to work past five o'clock and tried harder to be more present in the lives of those I love. Eventually, I left my job for another company that offered a little more freedom. I visit my family more, take time off when people need me, and my best friend and I can now have a weekly work share date to ensure we have time for each other. Now, as my current job begins to consume more and more of my time and I struggle with the fears of entrepreneurship, I find myself hearing Kurtis' voice reminding me that I will "succeed past my own expectations", encouraging me to pursue my own dreams.

On March 23, 2019 we laid him to rest in the field of honour in Edmonton, Alberta, beneath a waving Canadian flag. Waking that morning, the atmosphere was thick with heavy fog, as though the spirit world had descended into earth. By the time we arrived at the cemetery for his burial service, the fog was gone, and the sun was out, warm and golden as if the heavens were open above us. Laying my letter and a purple amethyst stone on top of the vault containing his ashes, I felt a charge of energy flow through me. If his mom hadn't already been holding me, I may have very well fallen to my knees. He'd finally been welcomed home to Valhalla where he belonged, and I think we all felt it happen.

Even though it has already been three years since he passed, his heart literally giving out from the weight of his burdens, many of us have said that it still feels like yesterday. I believe this is the impact felt when someone as deeply loved and admired as he was is taken too soon. Living in his truth and loving as openly as he did made him larger than life. It took three years for many of us to come to terms with his death and say our goodbyes in that field. Many of us still struggle with our guilt and regrets today - myself included.

Although there is much work to do to properly support our troops upon their return home to Canada, it is good to know our soldiers still have each other. His Commanding Officer, along with the RSM and Adam, one of his brothers, now a Sargent (1 CER, Task Force 3-09), ensured he was properly honoured with three Memorial Crosses, five Memorial Ribbons, a Memorial Bar and a Memorial Scroll. They are all great honours within the Military, and not to be taken lightly. Still learning about PTSD and the effects it has on our soldiers, I realize that what I experienced with Kurtis was only a drop in the ocean compared to what he and many of our soldiers experience. In my opinion, it is something that needs to be recognized and taken much more seriously in our country and by our government. While our soldiers are trained to be survivors of combat, they are struggling to survive the demons of PTSD, and some simply aren't making it at all. If you know someone with PTSD, check in on them. Be there for them. Let them know they are loved and cherished. While they have the courage to fight for our country and risk their lives doing so, returning home, they often lose the strength to continue fighting their inner war.

Rest in Peace, Cpl. Kurtis M. Gaucher.

AKA Lefty. Our "peg leg Pirate"

Thank you for being the man I needed.

Lest We Forget.

Acknowledgements: Miss Emily and Jack - Your Daddy loves you so much. He is so proud of you both. It goes without saying, to all of our service members, for all of your sacrifices made serving this Country - THANK YOU.

About the Author

Born in Ontario, Falon Malec grew up surrounded by the lakes and wilderness of the well-loved Muskoka region. Here she developed her love of the wild, raw beauty of our Mother Earth and all the creatures that live within her. Falon feels deeply connected to the planet and is instinctively attuned with both fauna and flora alike.

As a lover of the visual arts, Falon enjoys painting in her downtime and finds it to be extremely therapeutic, soulfully nourishing and intends to branch out into Art Therapy.

She has been a lover of books since she was a young child, so it is no surprise that she would eventually open herself to the possibilities of writing. Raw and authentic, she shares her passion for life and love, and explores her spirituality, sexuality and emotional discoveries in the relationships she has experienced through her blog, Life's Dirty Secrets.

Spiritually guided, she believes everything happens for a reason and is learning to trust the process and enjoy the journey the Universe has in store, while she creates The Goddess Guild, a community of sisterhood built on a foundation of collaboration over competition. Through this platform she intends to publish more books with the women she meets through divine intervention.

Blog : www.lifesdirtysecrets.com

Website : www.thegoddessguild.ca

IG : @lifes.dirty.secrets. | @the.goddess.guild

FB : @the.goddess.guild.community | @dirtysecrets2017

SELF LOVE

Self-love runs deeper than face masks and bubble baths. Although they may find themselves as a part of our self-care routine, the level of love we have for ourselves shows up in the thoughts we think, and in turn the actions we take. Words and actions of others can cut deep, and the scars can grow and spread over time spreading like weeds over our souls and blocking our own light. Relentless we must be in our journey to falling in love with ourselves, and letting our light shine bright.

Stephanie's story tells of a deeply wounded soul that presented itself as needing validation from others to confirm that she was in fact, enough. It's a story of a heart that confused love with attention, and attention with love. It's a beautiful journey of looking for love in all the wrong places, and eventually coming home to find the love within.

SELF LOVE

"I rejected myself so badly for 24 years of my life, I didn't even know who Stephanie was."

–Stephanie Goudreault

CHAPTER SIX

Being a Victim Was Too Easy

I'm Stephanie, a small town Ontario girl, and I mean really small town... and this is my story. At 22 years old in my fifth year of university, I had my first breakup. I mean my first real shitty, emotional, caught-him-with-another-girl, ugly cry breakup. And all I could think about is how badly I wanted him back, how I wouldn't survive without him, and how life would be miserable without my six-month-old relationship. I somehow felt comfort in a relationship that was wrong in every way, shape or form. I was blinded by the idea of having a boyfriend, a man I could trust, love and support. In the throes of my heartache, I found myself questioning everything. Why was I even taking this program? Why was I even here in Northern Ontario? While a voice boomed in my mind, "Don't be a university drop out, don't be a bum. Be the perfect Granddaughter!" It was the same voice that haunted me all throughout high school and pressured me to be top notch, or else. It was the voice of my grandfather. My grandfather was the one who had shown me at a very young age that men were manipulative, narcissistic and emotionless. Up until my early twenties, I sincerely believed that this was how they were designed. It was an incredibly distorted belief, yet that is all that I could see in most of the men in my life, so it must have been true. I didn't realize it at the time, but through the pain and upheaval of the heartbreak is really when my real journey began. I would put on a smile in the morning when I headed to class, but as soon as I was in my apartment in Sudbury, Ontario, I felt like I was dying on the inside. After the break-up, I hurled into a depression and it took all the willpower I had to do even the simplest things, like get out of bed. I would lie awake all night, and cry most of the day, feeling completely lost in who I was. I validated myself by what people thought of me, and being rejected was my worst nightmare. I started taking antidepressants because that's what my doctor told me to do. I had no real solution to any of this, and assumed that this was 'just life'. After all, my family was taking the medication, so I should probably do the same. That's how it's supposed to be right? This is hereditary, it's something I have to look forward to, whatever would take the pain away.

After I somehow made it through to graduation, I left my small-town Ontario life and moved to Halifax, Nova Scotia, as the warmer weather and the sea were calling my name. I was attracted to the old castle-like buildings, and the new province feels. I was free, in a new city with my best friend and no one here would even know who I was. I had no plans, and I had been feeling good on the medication. I started sleeping with different men, and enjoying the pleasure of sex since my family's reputation wasn't on the line anymore. Being from a small town, everyone knew my business before I did, and being the granddaughter of a successful local entrepreneur had its standards to uphold. As my new adventure started, I was going on date, after date, after date without any real luck in finding a real partner. So instead, I kept my company in sleeping with different guys so I wouldn't feel lonely, which, by no surprise, led me to feel the loneliest I had ever felt.

As this pattern of grasping at thin air for love and attention continued, it had slowly become my new normal to sleep with different men for comfort, even the married ones. My need for affection held no boundaries. At 22 years old, I didn't care about myself, so in turn I didn't care about the world. I didn't care who I could hurt along the way, I didn't care about the consequences, nor did I care if I lost myself throughout the journey. Rejected was my middle name. I was rejecting myself and in turn, I expected the same from men. This was a behaviour I learned, a pattern I fell deeply into, and one that I adopted like a champion. When I did find myself in a relationship (which was not very often), I would either catch them cheating or they would simply ghost me after a few months, rejected. This is the reality I had created. Were they really cheating on me? Or had I been cheating on myself by lowering my standards in a desperate attempt to feel loved by a man?

Throughout my life, I did what everyone else wanted me to do. I took dance, skating and piano lessons. I joined a soccer league and I enrolled in biomedical studies! I never once stopped to think, what does Stephanie really want to do? I discredited every single idea that came through my head, for fear of being rejected, laughed at or ridiculed. I was from a small town, living with the threatening stigma of life falling short after high school. Truth be told, I wanted to be an entrepreneur, get a master's degree in psychology, travel the world, and have millions of dollars that I could donate to animal welfare charities. I had big dreams! Yet I wouldn't allow myself to believe in them, and I certainly wouldn't share them with anyone. Nobody really knew the authentic me, so it became easier to fit myself into their comfort zones, especially Grandpa's.

As time went on, the reality was that I wasn't true to my-self. I was leaving my soul behind and I invited my misery with grace. I reverted back to my sleeping buddy, Rob, because, well, I knew he wouldn't leave me. As time went on without a real solid relationship, I felt inadequate and unworthy, and I judged myself harshly throughout the process. The relationship with myself never got any better, and at the time I couldn't figure out why. I was staying small in my decisions about life, about sex and about men, submitting to everything that was expected of me. I turned to carbs to kick the feelings of being unloved, uncared for and unwanted. I was filling the void, from the outside in.

They say if you're not paying attention, the lesson will eventually hit you like the broadside of a barn, well here was my wakeup call. I got a text message from Rob asking me if I was the one who had given it to him. 'It' being Chlamydia. My heart sank, and I started to cry. I puked in the bathroom with disgust as I branded myself as dirty and broken. I cried for a solid few hours after hearing the news that I too would need to get checked. Chances are, he said, I have it too. In fact, I did. Lucky enough, the Universe gave me a second chance because it was curable after all. The doctors were very nice, and assured me I was lucky that this infection was only temporary and advised me to take better care. Noted. I can assure you that this was the very first time in my life, I asked myself, "Stephanie, what are you doing?"

As the tidal wave of reality began to hit me, I started to see how I had allowed myself to be disrespected, to feel dirty, and become the loneliest I had ever felt in my life. I didn't know where to start in order to change my life. I needed to figure out what my next steps were and I realized how I knew little about myself, outside of sexual preference. Sheesh. So, I took a trip to where I felt the most valued and loved, to see my Mom and Grandmother in Northern Ontario.

By then, my Grandfather was in a nursing home and I hadn't seen him in months. I wasn't fully aware that his Dementia and Alzheimer's had gotten as bad as it had. In fact, when I walked in, I knew right then and there that he didn't recognize me or remember who I was. After all these years of frustration, anger, resentment and cries for his affection, he had stared at me like a complete stranger. I had spent a lot of time trying to relieve myself of the issues created by my grandfather, only to create a life where I relived them every single day. There I was, still finding myself craving his love and approval, and he no longer knew my name. Writing this now, I realize how messed up that is.

It's around that time that I heard about life coaches, and had been referred to one by a trusted source. He was the first man that I would truly confide in (without sleeping with). I knew that he could help me get through the pain, suffering and sabotage I had manifested into my life. This was the first man that I felt I could trust and simply be myself around. As months went on, he sincerely helped me release a lot of the pain I was holding so tightly to, and the story I was creating in my head about being unlovable or unworthy. The emotional abuse I had been through with my grandfather is all I could talk about. I blamed him for everything and when I say everything, I mean it. He wasn't a very nice man. He started calling me names before I was even in high school. He would be nice and supportive to me in public, but when we were at home and the door was closed, it was a different story. As the only granddaughter, he had high hopes and big dreams for me, ones that I would never achieve, and didn't want. As a little girl, all I wanted was to feel his love and his acceptance. I blamed him for all the abandonment issues, the fear of rejection, the people pleasing, and feeling inadequate and unworthy, the weight of which was preventing me from experiencing my own freedom and living a healthy life. I had to find a way to forgive my grandfather, so I could set myself free and live a happy and fulfilling life.

They say it gets harder before it gets easier, and I found that to be true. My life coach was in financial and relationship trouble, and needed a place to stay. Being the genuine, caring and generous person I am, I offered him my spare bedroom. Yup, not thinking clearly and feeling so grateful for his help and expertise, I thought it would be the perfect opportunity to return the favor. A few days turned into a week, then into a month and then into me financially supporting him. In hindsight now, I could see the pattern. I was feeling loved, when I was really being used. After my experience with men, was that a shocker? Nope. In fact, it validated all the fears I had around relationships and the opposite sex. You would think after being burned so many times that I would see these things coming from a mile away, but nope I continued to engage in unhealthy relationships and behaviours. Why? It was cyclical, and it felt like no matter how hard I tried, I ran towards the nearest man who made me feel wanted. With each encounter, grew a deep fear of forever being alone, single and abandoned. Every time I found myself alone in my condo or single at an event, it would trigger panic attacks. It was a double-edged sword because as a defense mechanism, I would isolate myself entirely for fear of feeling rejected, unloved and unworthy, but I was also afraid of being left out. I FINALLY made the corporate decision to stop dating, stop having sex and stop working. I ultimately fell apart at the seams hearing my Grandfather's voice in my mind, reaffirming what a failure I had become. As I sat there, curled in a ball hating who I had become, I got a phone call that would change my life, my grandfather was in palliative care, and only had a few days to live.

On January 17, 2017, my grandfather took his last breath, and I took my first one. His departure was like a release of my soul; the unleashing of the cage that had kept me stuck for so long. The feeling of complete freedom, it's like he had given me the strength I needed to become the best version of myself, and I believe it was his way of finally giving me the love that I had wanted from him so badly. It was that very night around the dinner table with my closest family members that I decided I wasn't going to do these panic attacks anymore, I wasn't going to have this stupid anxiety, and I definitely wouldn't allow my past to dictate how my future was going to unfold. I had been rejecting myself so much to please other people, that I created my own sick patterns. To me, it was easier to have a few "friends with benefits" knowing they would never leave, than to admit to myself that I wanted more. It was easier to feel numb and careless, than to be myself and feel out all my emotions. It was easier to feel unworthy, and inadequate because I didn't have to face the fact that I had given up on my dreams. And all these choices I had made allowed me to keep rejecting every slight possibility of a fruitful life. I rejected myself so badly for 24 years of my life that I didn't even know who Stephanie was anymore.

As I let go of the anxiety and started seriously diving into personal development, I found myself continuing to struggle with intimate relationships. What is going on? I'm doing the work, why isn't this working? I still felt unworthy, and therefore was attracting men who didn't value me in return. I recognized that I had serious body image issues, and in turn attracted men who saw me as easy. These men knew to capitalize on my pursuit of validation and short intervals of feeling beautiful and loved. But the truth is, I was avoiding doing the one thing that would truly change my circumstances: invite self-love. My focus no longer needed to be healing my wounds from my narcissistic Grandfather and I no longer needed to spend all of my energy finding love in all the wrong places. I had to devote everything I had to learning to love myself first. Unconditionally. Above all else.

When I finally decided to go off my antidepressant medication, all of the emotions I had been suppressing came flooding back. It was shocking for me, as I had grown so used to feeling so little for many years now. I had to fight my urges to give up on myself, because with the sudden influx of emotions, my instinct was to numb them the only way I knew how: sex (and sometimes carbs). It was the tool that I pulled from my toolbox the most frequently, the same way that some people turn to the bottle to escape the pain. But on the night of my grandfather's death, I had made a pact with myself to become the better version of myself, and most of all, to commit to loving myself through hell or high water, whatever it took. I had to slowly increase my emotional mastery, work on my mindset and protect my energy fiercely. It was the only way out of this dark pit I had built as a home for myself.

In my journey, forgiving myself was the hardest part of all. I had really let myself down. I had fallen so far into the depths of self-loathing that I couldn't wrap my head around how a smart and capable woman like myself could let herself create such a toxic environment. I couldn't blame anyone or anything anymore, not even

Grandpa. He wasn't my reason to stay stuck anymore. My healing and my forgiveness were on me, and I had to take responsibility for them. I was disappointed in myself, and I had to work incredibly hard and consistently to move from anger to compassion towards myself. Slowly over time, I began to rediscover myself. I had buried her pretty deep! The process of discovering who I am allowed me to love the process of life. The ups and downs, the highs and lows, the good and bad. It was all teaching me something, and in many ways, it all played a role in kicking me back to the path I was meant to be on. I guess I just decided to take the scenic route back home to me.

As this new journey had begun, I quickly realized that empowering other people gave me the energy I needed to empower myself, that helping people reach their highest goals kept me accountable to reach my own, and coaching other people to ultimately become the best versions of themselves helped me become the best version of myself. And that's all I needed, to strive every day to become the best version of Stephanie, and I knew right then and there that I had won this battle of being a victim.

Acknowledgements: Thank you to my mom and Nana for being my biggest cheerleaders, for the love and positivity you have modeled for me, and for being the sunshine to my rainy days. I love you always.

About the Author

Stephanie Goudreault is the tough love, no beating-around-the-bush type of empowerment teacher people need. She sees the best in people, and can empower them to see the same. She believes that we have complete power over our own reality, and that our emotional state is what manifests into our current life, which is meant to be lived with passion, fun, adventure and love. Stephanie spent most of her late teens and early twenties pleasing other people. She never felt like she could truly be herself, and was afraid of being too much. She set out on a path of downward spiral in her early twenties. Spending a few years in this dark world, she made a pact with herself that she would become the best version of herself and never feel this way again. It's through her own drive that she taught herself how to let go of her anxiety, relieve depression and cease her severe panic attacks. In pursuit of living her best life, Stephanie pursued various degrees trying to find what lit her soul on fire. Finally taking the plunge, she is a flight attendant turned personal empowerment teacher, author and business owner. Through her story, unique teaching methods, and programs, she has helped dozens of people connect with their emotions, transform their beliefs, empower their minds, gain an insane amount of confidence, and fall in love with life again. Stephanie has combined her passion for human potential and her God-given gift as a fierce empath to guide people in releasing emotional discomfort, and thriving in their daily lives.

www.stephaniegoudreault.com

Instagram: @stephanie.goudreault

Facebook @stephgoudreault

SURRENDER

To surrender means not to give up and wave the white flag, but rather to stop fighting against what inevitably is. It's letting go of the push, and falling into the flow. It's releasing the attachment we have for an outcome and accepting the journey for how it all unfolds. It's a deep knowing that we are taken care of, loved and supported no matter what the end result is. That amidst the pain of uncertainty, we allow a sense of peace and calm to take the lead.

Koa's story is one that many Canadian women experience. It's experienced in silence, in solitude, in confusion, and often in a sense of hopelessness. According to The Canadian Mental Health Association, one in five Canadians are directly impacted by mental health illness, and many more are indirectly affected. This is the inspiring story of a woman at war with herself, and her journey home to inner peace.

BECOMING MY OWN SOLUTION

*"I had to open my own doors, and shatter
my own ceilings."*

—Koa Hughes

CHAPTER SEVEN

Becoming My Own Solution

I believe that our biggest triumphs are born out of adversity. I didn't always believe this; it has actually taken me a significant amount of internal work to start seeing my so-called adversities and hardships as my true power. From the outside, my life is pretty damn great. Most people who know me, only know the things about me that they can see on the outside, but no one really knows what I have been through, to get me to where I am today. I am always getting compliments on my wonderful life, it seems that people see my life with nice green grass and a little white picket fence. Standing on the outside of that little white picket fence, people can see that I have an amazing, attractive, successful husband and two happy, healthy children. My husband and I are entrepreneurs, and we co-own a well-established, award-winning construction company. Just this past year, my family and I were featured on a CBC TV documentary, The Stats of Life, where we were able to showcase some parts of our life as entrepreneurs. I have people tell me that they envy me because I have the privilege of being a published author; I am currently writing as a co-author in two books. I post beautiful pictures with inspirational quotes on my social media, and it looks like I have it all together. I might have nice green grass, and a cute little white picket fence, but my foundation has been cracked over and over again, and in reality, the entire structure could crumble on any given day. It is so easy to make assumptions about another person's seemingly "picture perfect" life, and forget that there is a history that got them to where they are now. If you had met me five or more years ago, you would have come face-to-face with a defeated, abused, uneducated, depressed, suicidal, woman, with no career, no dreams, no car, no house, and no real life goals, other than to keep my children alive.

I remember the exact moment that I realized something was seriously wrong with me. I was having a panic attack, sobbing, hyperventilating, driving to my mother's house to pick up my children. In the moment, it took every ounce of effort I could muster, to not swerve my truck at full speed, off the side of the mountain or into oncoming traffic. I wanted to die so badly. But my children needed me. That was the one and only thing that stopped me, and took me to the doctor instead. I wasn't honest with my medical team about what I was feeling because I was too ashamed to admit what my life had been like for the past three months. I couldn't tell my doctor that for three months I had drank almost a 26-ounce bottle of vodka every single day. I couldn't tell her that I was only sleeping three hours a night, and full of energy, because that seemed crazy. I couldn't tell her that I spent all the money in my bank account, and my ex's bank account, and ate up our savings. I couldn't tell her that I was so caught up in having sexual relationships with any man that I could get, that I was failing to be a good mother to my children. It is still painful just to admit that. I couldn't tell my doctor that despite my children making it to school, although late, and being fed, I neglected the physical and emotional needs of my children, and they withdrew into their own little worlds to escape my instability. No, I sure as hell couldn't tell my doctor that. What would she think of me? So I didn't tell her. I only told her I was depressed. After the panic set in about what I had done and how I had behaved for the past three months, my mood went from happy, high, and excited, to the lowest I have ever felt. Because I was too ashamed to be honest with my doctor, I was improperly diagnosed with Major Depressive Disorder and anxiety. I took my cocktail of new antidepressant medications, sleeping pills, Ativan and anxiety medication, packed myself and my kids up, and took us to my mother's. The thoughts of those past three months plagued me. I couldn't stop crying. I couldn't sleep without heavily medicating myself, or cuddle my children, because I was harbouring so much guilt about what I had just put them through. We stayed in my mother's basement because I was too scared to be alone with myself and my kids. It took a few months, but I made it out of that dark, terrifying hole, and within a few months, I took another ride on up to my happy, high and excited self. The mania.

(Q

I pride myself on being an educated woman. I went to university and earned a degree in psychology and indigenous studies. During my periods of normalcy, I was aware that something was wrong with my mental health. Despite my education, I ignorantly ignored the signs. For years my moods cycled up and down. My depression would make me withdrawn, angry, sad, tired, unmotivated, and difficult to deal with. My manic moods would make me energetic, happy, full of life, full of big ideas and plans, and I felt like I was so much fun! But it isn't all fun and happiness, the mania also would make me irritable, irrational, judgmental, unpredictable, and unstable. It took me until I was in my thirties to finally understand what I was doing to myself, my children, and my now husband.

I wish I had known sooner. Now that I understand my disease, I understand that it started when I was a teenager. I was in so much turmoil as a teenager that my final year of high school was Grade 9, during which I spent most of my time skipping class. I was failing, and so far behind on my work that I didn't think I would ever be able to get caught up. When I dropped out of high school, I ran away from home and moved to another province. My parents never came to get me. During this time, I survived by working odd jobs and couch surfing. I lived a high risk lifestyle for most of my teen years. To be honest, I did what I needed to do to get by, which usually meant going from boy to boy, house to house, and job to job - whatever was necessary to have a place to stay and food to eat. I drank daily and smoked so much marijuana because I couldn't cope with my mental and emotional health. The only thing that brought me home at 16 years old was a teenage pregnancy, an abortion and nowhere else to go. Moving back in with my Mom didn't make anything easier. My mom was struggling with her own mental health issues, she couldn't keep a full-time job, she was depressed, she couldn't manage to keep the house clean, or bills paid. I had to find a job, and help my mom pay her bills, and I found myself in the same mess of drinking, bad relationships, and spiraling mental health.

When I was 20 years old, my son came into my life and I knew that something had to change. I had no high school education, and I would need to actually put in some work if I ever wanted a better job. This is the very beginning of when I started to have an urge for more in life. I was sure that changing my physical environment would fix all of my problems. I applied to do my upgrading at the local college. Within two years, I was accepted into university, in the Bachelor of Arts program, and given entrance scholarships for my hard work. I had to parent, work full-time and still attend school. Parenting was hard for me. I had postpartum depression, and anxiety, and struggled with keeping my still untreated Bipolar Disorder in check. Despite my out-of-control mental health, I completed a double major in psychology and indigenous studies. It took me a lot longer to finish my degree than most of my fellow students, because I was busy caring for a toddler; I also welcomed another child into my life mid-way through my studies. It was after my second child came into my life, and a very dark postpartum depression set in, that I realized I desperately needed support. Medications for depression and counselling didn't fully cut it, and I realized that I wasn't getting the support at home that I required. Up until this point, I didn't know that I was in an emotionally abusive relationship with a narcissist. Holy shit, how did I not see it before? How the hell had I found myself in an abusive relationship? Again, I had prided myself on being an educated woman, and I couldn't accept my own reality. I kept telling myself that I should have known better. The scary thing about narcissistic abuse is that it damages your ability to feel any kind of self-worth or to even feel competency in your own mind. Emotional abuse brings you down to such a low place that you become certain that you deserve everything you are getting, and that you are the cause of the abuse. I was exhausted, alone, and struggling with my untreated mental illness. I was so ready for a change, but leaving an abusive situation like mine wasn't as easy. It took about two years of planning my escape before it was possible, not because of fear but because of the complete control he had over my life and finances. Leaving required me to hide money, secretly apply for jobs, and buy and store furniture at other people's houses before I actually made my move. The combination of the stress of leaving my abuser, and starting new anti-depressants and anti-anxiety medication is what threw me into my worst manic episode to date. What was supposed to be the start of my new, happy life after finally escaping the abuse, turned into a living hell.

So there I was, five years ago, fresh off a manic high, single, broke, medicated, depressed, living in my mother's basement, sharing an air mattress with both kids, still refusing to admit my mental illness. At that time, I still believed so many limiting beliefs about myself; I believed that I wasn't enough and never would be. I still didn't feel that my mind was competent, and my self-worth was non-existent. I was convinced that I would never become anyone of any importance in this world. I believed that if I admitted my mental illness, I would be seen as unstable and incompetent. What if someone took away my children? What would people think of me? How would I be judged? I didn't want to be the crazy one. I held onto this disempowering and limiting mindset up until I met my husband - he helped me change my perspective, and he helped me find treatment for my mental illness. Sometimes we can only turn our challenges into inspiration once we have received the support we need to finally see that we are responsible for making our life happen. I needed someone to help me see that I could create a new story for myself. I had always seen my adversities and my mental health as major setbacks, and I had accepted the fate that I was going to be screwed up forever. The moment that I started to use my adversity as my own empowerment, my life changed. My husband didn't fix everything for me, but he taught me that I had the power to create the life that I wanted, be the person that I wanted to be, and that I was capable. I might not be able to cure my mental illness, but I now understand that I was the problem in my own life, and I had to become my own solution.

Seeing a psychiatrist and finally being diagnosed with Bipolar 2 Disorder changed my life for the better. When I heard the words "I am fairly certain you have Bipolar 2

Disorder," I laughed. I actually left the office, laughing. I couldn't stop laughing. I called my husband, and told him, all while laughing. I kept thinking "finally it all makes sense." I was manic at this time, and feeling high on life, and so I went to the gym, and sat in the steam room, and my laughing turned into sobbing. My life needed to change. I had so many thoughts swirling in my mind: lifelong medication, disease of the brain, no cure, the mood swings will never truly stop, lifelong management. It was a lot to take in and it took me a few weeks of feeling sorry for myself to finally start to learn about my disease. I had a ton of work to do on myself.

What I have learned is that it is not the events of life that matter, but rather the meaning that we create from those events, empowering or disempowering. I had to choose to create a new meaning for my life by choosing to be empowered because of the adversity I have been through. I refuse to take the backseat in my own life, and instead I have to make the choice every single day to remain the driver. I may have a brain disease that I will have to live with for the rest of my life, but I will not let that define me. I am not my mental illness. And if you are like me, and need support to turn your chal-lenges, or the struggles that are a part of your mental illness, into your own inspiration, I am here to be your support and tell you that you can learn to be resilient, you can learn to be proactive in your life, you can learn to believe in yourself, and you can create a new story for yourself.

Learn to be resilient. Resilience is not something that is just innate; it requires learning and developing new behaviours, thoughts and actions. Resiliency is a process of thriving through adversity, trauma, tragedy and significant stress. People with bipolar disorder, or any major mental health illness, have to pick themselves up again and again. Sometimes you have to start from scratch. Through resiliency, I have taught myself to not focus on the difficult times, many of which could have broken me, but rather to pay attention to and learn to embrace the actions that I took in order to get through the difficult times. Becoming resilient requires work though, because I fully believe that in order to be successful in life, you have to be proactive in your own life every single day.

Take a proactive approach. We have two choices when we are facing some kind of adversity. We can take action and do something about it, or we can just wait until it inevitably arrives on our doorstep. I learned the hard way, and waited until my problems were banging down my door. When I finally sought treatment for my mental health, I was terrified to be labelled as the woman with Bipolar Disorder. My psychiatrist told me that how well I function will be a direct result of how smart I am with treating my illness. I have taken that to heart, and applied it to my daily life. To be honest, very few people know that I suffer daily from this illness, and that is because of how proactive I have been in managing my symptoms and my daily life. Every single day, I follow my treatment plan, and I am proactive in my mental health self-care. You may hear it all the time: get enough sleep, eat a healthy diet, get daily exercise, and take time for self-care. Sometimes those things seem so hard. I used to put my own health on the back burner. I was too busy caring for my family and worrying about everyone and everything else. But let me tell you, when you do not take a proactive approach to your body, mind, and soul, you will never be able to be the best version of yourself. Every day that I was sleeping too little, or substituting coffee for food, or working myself to death, I was robbing myself of the opportunity to be mentally well, which means robbing my family of having a mentally-well mother and partner. Being proactive is essential in having an empowered, happy, healthy life.

Change your limiting beliefs and start believing in yourself. I know what that voice in your head says: "You can't do it. You're going to fail. You will never be good enough." I know that voice so well. It is the voice that taunts me whenever I set a goal. It criticizes me when life gets difficult, and if you are like me, you have probably spent more time being your own worst enemy. Know this: you deserve to treat yourself better, and you deserve to believe in yourself. No matter how proactive you try to be, or how resilient you say you are, if you don't actually believe in yourself, your ability to overcome, and your ability to achieve the new standards you are now setting for yourself, you will fail. Our beliefs about our own self shape every action, thought and feeling that we experience; changing our belief system is critical to making any real change. In order to make lasting change, we have to start to truly believe that we are the solution to our own problems. I might not be able to find a permanent solution to my mental illness, that is something that will be with me forever; however, I am able to be a solution in managing my illness. You may not be able to control everything, but you can control how to respond to everything.

When I sit and reflect now, I always try to remind myself of how far I have actually come. We cannot forget where we came from, no matter how difficult those memories can be, because that adversity is what got us to where we are today; all of those things happened for us, not to us. If you struggle with adversity and self-doubt, let me say to all of you that tomorrow is a new day. A new day to change your path. A new day to pick yourself up. A new day to start over. A new day to trust that you are competent and capable. A new day to choose to create empowered meaning in your life.

How will you start to use all of your challenges and adversity to help you birth new triumphs? Beautiful Woman, ask yourself what is it that you really, truly want in life? You must believe that no matter what your past holds, you have it within you to make your future anything you want it to be because you are the solution to all of your own problems.

Acknowledgements: To my husband, Duffy, thank you for opening my eyes and my soul to what is possible in this life.

About the Author

Koa Hughes is an author, writer, mental health advocate, mentor, executive and entrepreneur. Through writing and mentorship, Koa strives to change the stigma and outlook for men and women who suffer from mental illness.

Koa has a Bachelor of Arts Degree, with a double major in psychology and indigenous studies. Koa is a published author in two co-author series, as well as a mental health advocate blogger. When Koa isn't writing and advocating, she is also busy at her day job as an executive entrepreneur. She owns an award-winning construction company with her husband. Koa and her family were featured on the CBC Television series The Stats of Life - Working Life.

Koa uses her education and her own mental illness diagnosis to help her better understand how to help women face and overcome their own adversity. Adversity is something Koa knows all too well: before becoming an author and executive, she had been lost; hopelessly adrift in a sea of abuse, trauma, limiting beliefs and untreated mental illness. An unhappy combination of medication and booze kept her afloat. Through immense growth, Koa has overcome huge obstacles. In order to live her best life, Koa made the choice to become her own solution.

FB: Koa Hughes

IG: @koabri

LOVE

Love isn't loud, messy and passionate. It's silent, peacefully present and unconditional. A mother's love is the purest love. A love that knows no bounds and accepts no limits. Her heart beats to the rhythm of her child's world. Her heart feels pain when her child feels pain. And her heart threatens to stop, when her child's heart stops. A love like this takes up so much room in a mother's heart, that when a child is lost, a deep void is left behind. A hole. A hole that can only be filled with love.

Brenda's story is one of tragedy, heartache and loss. And it's also a beautiful journey of love, hope and dedication. In the dark, toxic world of homicide, surviving means simply to place one foot in front of the other, and keep moving forward. Love means allowing your own heart to continue beating.

*"My broken heart continued to beat and
my lungs continued to expand.
I was alive and needed to decide how to live
without my boy."*

—Brenda Wiese

CHAPTER EIGHT

Life After Murder:

A Mother's Journey

I danced. I danced and I danced and I danced. As I twirled about, I could feel the shift. I could feel the shedding of my heavy coat of grief. I could feel the permission being granted. Permission to release the guilt of living, the guilt of the possibility of moving forward, the guilt of surviving, the guilt of finding a way to live after losing my son. It has been 18 months since my son Brett was murdered. It has been 18 months since I had felt true joy. That night, I gave myself permission to live again. For when I am living, I feel the closest to my son.

The death of a child is most certainly one of the most profound and painful losses the human spirit can endure. Without a doubt, I once believed that my heart would stop beating should one of my precious children die before me. Shockingly, this is not true! My broken heart continued to beat and my lungs expanded with air, and minutes ticked by and days turned to months. I was alive and I needed to decide how to live without my boy, but how was I going to rebuild and adapt to such a catastrophic loss?

(Q

At 9:40am on January 12, 2013, I was in the basement when I heard my husband calling my name and telling me to come upstairs. As I made my way up the stairs I saw a glimpse of the yellow stripe on the RCMP officers pant leg. In that split second my heart stopped. My life as I knew it, ended. By the time I got to the top of the stairs, I knew my son was dead. I'm not sure if someone said those words but I knew in my soul, my boy was gone. He had been stabbed to death.

I was living in a nightmare. I wanted my son. I needed my son. I was frozen and robotic for several weeks as I struggled to find my bearings. Nothing was normal. Nothing made sense. Time stood still. My days were long and I felt so unhooked, so detached, so shattered, so broken. My mouth was dry and I couldn't eat, yet all my body wanted to do was throw up. I desperately wanted to feel better, but I just couldn't. I couldn't feel anything other than deep, deep pain. In an attempt to regain some sort of alternative sensation, we had our massage therapist come to our home. As she was progressing with my massage, she expressed concern about how cold I was and kept piling blankets on me. I realized then that my body was working overtime to shunt all my blood to my heart and brain in a desperate attempt to keep me alive.

Several weeks after our tragic news, in a moment of courage, I thought I was ready to start going back to yoga, thinking it would be a safe place to start moving my body. I needed to move my body. My heart and soul needed me to. As I connected to my mat, I recall with great clarity how vulnerable I felt. It felt impossible to focus and I struggled to keep my emotions at bay as I flowed through my practice. I had an overwhelming feeling of Brett's presence, like he was there with me in the studio. I was overcome by visions of my baby boy when he was born, and how much love he had flooded my heart with. He was my baby boy. My son. I left the yoga mat that evening with tears flowing down my face and a deep sense of emotion brewing from within, one I had not yet felt to this magnitude. I had an uncontrollable urge to listen to the music that we would play to settle him to sleep at night when he was a baby. I desperately wanted to feel my son's presence. When I got home I searched through his baby stuff and found the precious cassette tape. I knew there was an old cassette player in the storage room in the basement, so I took the tape to the basement and frantically put it in the player and pressed play. The moment the music began to play, I was hit by a wave of emotion and grief and the flood gates opened. There I lay on the cold cement floor, yearning so deeply for my baby that I thought my body would explode. There's no possible way this level of pain can stay contained in one body. I cried so loudly, moaning from the pain, and it ran deep. I wept and I wept as the music played on. My husband, who was also grieving the loss of our son, finally came downstairs and gently convinced me to come to bed. The music stopped, but my grief didn't. The emotional tidal wave continued throughout most of the night as the tears continued to rain down my face and my heart felt like it would explode at any moment. Again, my body was working incredibly hard to keep me alive.

The next day, my was face was so swollen that I could barely open my eyes. Through tiny slits I saw myself in the mirror and I thought maybe this was it. Maybe I had hit bottom and I wouldn't recover. Part of me was terrified and part of me was at peace, like I was accepting that it made sense for a mother who has had her baby ripped away from her to feel this magnitude of grief. Somehow, by the grace of God, or by the power of my son, I eventually rose up and took steps forward into my day. I knew that if I had managed to survive the night, my grief would not kill me. I decided to trust myself fully to pull through this horrendously painful journey. I learned that when I allowed myself to surrender to my debilitating grief, it could be painful, profound and powerful all at the same time. I had to trust my innate ability to open my heart, despite how relentlessly it was trying to slam shut out of pure self-preservation. I knew that this was where my growth and healing would begin. Hope had appeared for the first time.

Journal Entry: October 22, 2013

On our way home from Maritimes. Read the book called "I'll see you again" by Jackie Hance. Her three children were killed in July 2009. Her sister in law was driving drunk. The book was profound in what it offered me. Her words resonated with me. She validates my feeling and thoughts that I have had over the last 9 months. Acknowledging the powerful and debilitating grip that grief can have. She is evidence of how LOW and broken the human spirit can be and yet there is hope. Hope for one day having a peaceful life, with moments of joy and fulfillment. That one day I will be able to have a warm, loving feeling as I remember having and cherish all my memories of Brett and the life we had as a family. Instead of feeling like my heart, soul and body are going to EXPLODE! A pain so great that I could throw up. A pain so great that I'm sure my heart is going to stop! Jackie Hance is living proof that there is HOPE. I feel so hopeless at times and yet a part of me trusts that I will get to that peaceful place, I have always felt deep within myself that I have potential to get to that elusive place. I am surprised that I have an inner strength that I did not believe would be possible. I have such a DEEP, endless, powerful love for my children. I have always believed that I would absolutely die if one of them died before me, this was unquestionable to me prior to Jan 12. I am surprised and shocked at how capable and strong I actually am. I've thought many times that this inner, unknown strength is coming from a sort of Divine power, perhaps my precious boy himself is holding me up with God's guidance. I know very clearly what I want for myself...my wish for me is: I want a peaceful, content, loving heart. I want to feel joy, compassion and unconditional acceptance. I want to submit to my grief and accept what has happened and to trust in a higher power that I did not cause what happened, nor could I have ever controlled what happened. I want to believe that we are all spiritual beings having a human experience and that my JOB here on earth is to do my best, be my best and to learn 100% self love and acceptance. To trust and accept that others are responsible for their choices and their own life path, as I am responsible for my life path. I want to one day be able to be free from the anger and hatred I feel for [the accused] and their families. I truly want to have nothing invested in them or in their life choices, decisions or path they chose. I find power in that...that if I can get to that state then it's like I am 'unlinking' Brett from them. It's freeing Brett and the rest of us from these people who thrust us onto a path that we had NO choice in, no control over. I want to be able to have FUN... Right now the best it can be is some enjoyment. I want to be able to have free, uninhibited fun, to laugh from my belly, to feel free! I want to feel that I deserve freedom, contentment and joyfulness. I want to have openness and love and fun and joy with my husband. And equally as important, I want to see Jody and Morgan have joy, fun and peace too. I want them to have life goals and aspirations. I want all of us to live with passion and purpose. I want to watch my beautiful daughter step in this world and LIVE wholeheartedly and to be the person she is meant to be! I don't want to be living at 20%...carrying a coat of grief everyday, every second. I want to be able to have clarity of purpose. I want confidence to make a difference in this world. I want to take this horrific life experience and help people, to make a positive contribution to our society. I pray for clarity of my mind, my inner soul to see the signs of where I can make a difference and HOW I can make a difference. THIS is my wish for me!

But how? How was I going to keep moving forward to-wards peace and joy? After surviving the lowest of lows on this grief journey and reading Jackie Hance's story, I knew it was up to me. I knew I had the strength and dedication to work towards a new life with peace and joy. I knew that is what Brett would want for his Momma because it is who I was before he was murdered, and I needed to honour him by living my best life with grace and peace. The ugly truth about homicide is that through the court system, my family and I would be forced to relive the nightmare with each new hearing or appeal. Knowing that we would be required to face our heartache head-on, over and over again made it all the more critical I strengthen my own foundation. I started my healing journey by becoming crystal clear on what is medicine to my heart and to my soul. I began exercising and eating nutritious foods. I became more protective of my time, and implemented boundaries. I spent time with those who cheered me on and distanced myself from those who stole from my limited energy reserve. I created a balance between solitude and being social. I began spending more time in nature with my horse. These are the choices I had to make every single day. One foot in front of the other.

Journal Entry: January 28, 2019

We finally got home after 4 long days in the court-room... AGAIN! It's January 2019 it's the pretrial hearing where the lawyers argue before the Justice what evi-dence is admissible in the upcoming retrial, which is now 3 months away. A RETRIAL...we have to go through this again for a third time, plus two preliminary hear-

ings. As we began our 2 hour drive north from Calgary to our home...our sanctuary, I had a feeling of relief that I will be sleeping in my own bed tonight. Calgary used to be our favourite city. We lived there for several years and our daughter was born there. Brett loved Calgary and this was where he met several very special friends. Calgary was the city of dreams for our family. But now it is plagued with horrible memories and we feel a sense of dread when there, especially when in the Northwest quadrant of the city. The majority of the drive home both Jody and I sit quietly, each processing the week's events, reflecting or just being still. Blank. Being in that world of courtroom proceedings, violence and crime fills us with frigid cold toxicity. In an effort to compartmentalize the events for self preservation, it feels like our physical bodies take the brunt of it, leaving us tired, quiet, still and in need of decompression. On our drive home, as we leave the city in our rear view mirror, the thawing process begins. I allow myself to start to slowly feel again. I allow myself to step back in-to my own life again, and I know from all the other times we left the city under very similar circumstances, that it is I who must make this effort to transition. I can't stay in that frozen, detached place even though it would be so easy to stay there, but I know deep in my soul this is not the place to live.

That same night I had a fitful, restless sleep and woke up from a dream about my Brett. He came to me as his ten-year-old self and told me not to worry, that he is with me and will never leave. These dreams are so con-flictual for me. I'm grateful on one hand that he was with me and that for that brief nanosecond I was whole again, my baby was with me, I could see him, touch him, feel him. Then I wake up and reality strikes, bringing a tidal wave of emotion along with it. All morning I was distraught, emotional, my heart heavy with deep sadness. Both my husband and I felt flat, completely exhausted and numb, but we made a choice to get up and move. We forced ourselves to put our boots on and head for the river; a place we have walked many times before. As I walked I observed a familiar feeling, like there was a tight belt around my chest that made it difficult to breathe. It felt like my shoes were cement, because even walking was taking a lot of effort. My husband kept saying, "Just keep putting one foot in front of the other." We trudged forward one step at a time. Slowly, minutes ticked by and eventually the tightness and heaviness relented and I started to enjoy my beautiful surroundings. I was breathing in clean, crisp Alberta winter air. The oxygen was reaching the bottom of my lungs and fueling my exhausted muscles. My heart was pumping, circulating clean blood cleansing myself of the courtroom filth. I could hear birds and see the beautiful frost hanging on the trees. I realized my protective armour was starting to melt away and I was slowly entering back into my beautiful world. I was living in colour again. With every step I was propelling myself forward. I was transfusing myself with light and oxygen which was such a contrast to the world I was in just 24 hours earlier; a world of darkness and toxicity. After this empowering walk, it occurred to me that I have done this exact thing, walking, trudging forward since the day Brett was killed. I'm still walking six years later and the truth is, I will continue to trudge forward for the rest of my life. Sometimes the walk will be light and airy, and sometimes it is going to be me hauling a heavy load of grief and pain. Every day, Brett is with me cheering me on. One foot in front of the other. One day at a time.

Acknowledgements: I'd like to thank my husband, Jody, and daughter, Morgan, for supporting me on this journey of healing, as we all transcend the darkness in search of peace and joy. My ultimate gratitude extends to my precious son, Brett, who will forever exist within the sacred space of my soul.

About the Author

Brenda Wiese has always lived her life from a strong foundation focusing on family, friends, and community. Growing up in central Saskatchewan with her four brothers, where her father farmed and her mother worked full-time as a nurse, family, freedom, nature, and animals were the four pillars of her youth. Brenda and her husband Jody raised two beautiful children, Brett and Morgan, in central rural Alberta, also valuing those same pillars she grew up with. She had no idea how significant those pillars would one day become, as she desperately fought to rebuild her shattered heart after her near perfect life came crashing down when two police officers knocked on her door with the news that would be every parent's worst nightmare: her 20-year-old son Brett had been murdered while at a private house party with his university friends. Her life has been a struggle as she finds her way through the blackness of grief, eventually adapting to a new normal and learning to live with a fractured soul. Discovering how to manage and survive the insane reality of homicide has been overwhelming and soul crushing, yet Brenda strives to make her son proud as she continues to live her life with grace, vulnerability and authenticity. She has deep gratitude for having been blessed with the privilege and honour of being Brett and Morgan's Momma!

SELF-ACCEPTANCE

To accept ourselves is to fully receive ourselves as we are. Self-acceptance is seeing ourselves through the eyes of grace, compassion and forgiveness. It is in how we choose to be gentle with ourselves, knowing our hearts and souls can be both strong and delicate simultaneously. Accepting ourselves is honouring ourselves in our most natural, real and raw state. Come what may, in whatever way, shape or form, but nothing will change our beauty inside and out, for we know who we are.

Barbara's story is one of a woman's journey in finding her way back home to herself. There was a deep inner knowing that she had remained hidden for far too long, and the residue of that pain was mirrored back to her in the eyes of her children. This story is a reminder for all that it is never, ever too late to grow.

MY CHILDREN WERE THE MIRROR I NEEDED

"Weird is the new normal"

–Barbara McBryer

CHAPTER NINE

My Children Were the Mirror I Needed

Life is full of surprises and no one thing can ever prepare us fully for what is to come on our journeys, especially if you didn't even realize you were on a journey in the first place. A lot of my life was spent simply existing. I didn't have conscious thoughts of knowing, with certainty, what I wanted to be. I didn't have any passion for anything in particular, nor any big dreams. I had only ever wished to be happy, as though it was something that would just happen one day, like magic. I didn't realize then that being happy is a choice. And I didn't discover it was a choice until I had started my parenting journey.

In my younger years, I didn't really feel engaged in life. Even though I was painfully shy in big groups and around people I didn't know, I still managed to march to the beat of my own drum. I had a fear of being seen or criticized for being weird, but at the same time I was also able to adapt to my environment, attempting to feel like I fit in with a variety of different groups. I had a quirky, and awkward sense of humour that I felt most didn't understand. I was a beautiful blend of smart and ass (smartass, get it?). I liked to tell stories with a dramatic flair - likely for a laugh, but mostly only around people I knew well. Sometimes my humour was sarcastic and biting, but that didn't matter as I had adopted this take-it-or-leave-it attitude. At the time, I had not realized that what I was doing was protecting myself by living in a bubble that very, very few people had permission to enter. It kept me safe from criticism. When I was in my bubble, I could be myself. It made me the one with the power so I wouldn't get hurt or made fun of and as a result, I would lash back with a sharp tongue if anyone challenged me. In retrospect, I believe that I was longing to feel understood and yearning to feel accepted.

I thought I was easy-going enough. I loved going out and dancing, and I enjoyed having a good time. I didn't understand why I had a hard time drawing good relationships to me. I didn't understand why I was repeating the same patterns. I did realize, in my mid-to-late twenties, that although I'd formed great female friendships, the party lifestyle I had adopted was superficial and a way to numb myself. I put myself in unsafe situations and I was using alcohol to give me courage, while allowing relationships to be in my life that were less than kind. I look back on those days now and wonder, "Who was that girl who so clearly couldn't stop running from the pain?" I started to make small changes in my life, such as less drinking and not dating, so I could make clearer decisions.

It wasn't until I had my first child, and I had a little person to keep safe and guide, that a bigger shift started. When she was a baby, I felt a strong connection to her; I was enamoured with this little person, she was always happy and it seemed so effortless. She was seemingly fearless. It was then that I realized I had never experienced true happiness. It created a sudden memory jolt within me about my birthdays or when I'd see a shooting star, and I remembered wishing to be happy. Her presence in my life jarred me, but in a good way because I was able to finally see that this lack of true happiness and purpose within me was going to have to change, if I was going to be able to raise my daughter to continue being the happy person she was when she came into this world.

With the birth of each of my three children, an even deeper shift would happen. Having my kids is what finally allowed me to see myself. They were like little mirrors, each of them reflecting a different part of me ever so clearly for the first time. That was what made me realize that I not only needed to change, but I wanted to change. I wanted to feel better. I wanted to choose happiness. They showed me something I couldn't see in myself, something I forgot, but was starting to know, was still inside of me. I consciously knew I could make better choices so I could protect them and in return, they protected me. Intellectually, I understood this but I wanted to step up in ways I believe I couldn't before. Even though I still had a fear of being seen, I wanted to advocate for my kids. You see, I thought when they got to school age, I would just drop them off, tell them to have a good day and they would have a good day. To my naive surprise, it wasn't that simple. They had bad days too, as they each began to face their own hardships. The bullying, because they were "weird". The teachers who didn't always know how to teach kids who learn differently. The lack of support for a child navigating the terrifying landscape of anxiety. I could feel their pain, and having not fully healed my own, I knew that I had work to do if I was going to be the pillar of strength they needed when they got home from school each day. If I was going to advocate for their individuality and their differences, I needed to first accept me for who I was, and become the role model they needed.

So as the kids grew, it felt like I was trying to grow too and, as I would kiss them goodbye each morning, I remember asking myself, How can I raise you to know yourself, if I don't even know myself? I had fallen into a rut of merely existing through the day-to-day drudgery. You know, the wake-up, cook, prepare, organize, commute, work, commute, cook, clean, sleep (maybe), repeat, repeat, repeat! Up until this point, it had all been routine, and I was growing entirely bored, angry and frustrated. Where was the fun, funky mum with a dramatic flair, animated gestures and odd facial expressions? There were hints of her, but her appearances were far and few between in those days. I knew she was there, but she was hiding. It had been so long since I had seen my true self in my own reflection, that I knew my journey of self-discovery was going to be a long one, and probably a little painful. In my fight for what I knew I needed to do for myself, I knew I also needed to do it for my kids. They needed a happy mother. A confident mother. A role model for themselves to look to for reaffirmation that being weird and unique and individual is totally cool and rad and awesome. Sigh. So where was I to even begin?

I'll tell you what would have been nice – if I had discovered personal development prior to having kids. It took the millennials to figure this one out, that it's better to find out who we really are before popping out three kids like I did (those smart millennials *insert eyeroll here*). In reality, though, I didn't think there was anything wrong with who I was, or that anything needed to change. But what I was attached to was the power that my reactive nature gave me. It was a way for me to feel big and strong because I'd been belittled for so many years, silenced by abusers. As painful as it felt, I started to really delve into healing myself. Why wasn't I happy? Why was I so reactive? Reactivity isn't always the best quality as a mum, or potentially as a person in general, unless your two-year-old child grabs a barbeque lighter and sets their hair on fire - that is a time to react! Or when one (or all) of my kids was called weird. I wanted to reframe, and take the sting out of the word to empower them. I would start to see this trend among their peers. Everything was so black and white for them. If it wasn't "cool" it was "weird." If we look at the definition of weird as meaning something that you don't know how to feel about yet, we can start to see that throughout history, the negative association of weird has created great divisions in our culture. There was something about empowering my children to see that being weird or different was an opportunity to further explore something within themselves. This opened me up to reconnect with the weird within me. In order to show my kids that weird is something that can be celebrated, I had to learn to celebrate the weird within me. I had to stop blending in, which meant I had to release the "taskmaster" approach to life and connect to playing again. Playing, after all I had been through, after all the years of my protective bubble-making, felt really foreign and unproductive. I had to see that I could hold my own value, without having to have everything planned and figured out all the time. Woah, so many realizations! All of this forced me to evolve and become a forager and gatherer of knowledge and skills that would help my children when others couldn't or wouldn't. I had to adapt and figure out how my kids were best able to learn. I took courses on the Davis Dyslexia method because my middle dude learned math easier with balls of clay than with numbers on a board. If my youngest wanted to grow a rat tail even when it's not in fashion, I would support his right to do so, because individuality and being unique should be nurtured in our children. Plus, let's be real: it's only hair and kids deserve to know that they have control over their bodies too. When my child needed moral support to talk through a panic attack, I would drop everything to get down into the pit with them. When my child was being accused of bullying, I'd have an honest conversation with him to discover that it was really retaliation out of frustration. So I'd speak up for him because no one else was willing to listen. When my child needed me to take them to an appointment across town, I did so without question.

So what did all this self-discovery business really do for me? It allowed me to really step into my own, in a new way. Still to this day, this is a work in progress, but as I softened and surrendered to the woman I was becoming who didn't need to hold onto the hard-to-touch exterior, I could feel that embracing my weird, my out-of-this-world sense of humor, could lead me to the community of women who accepted me for who I was, because I was allowing myself to show up as who I was for the first time in my entire life. These were relationships that were based on vulnerability and courage, and friendships that started from growth and light-heartedness, without the need to impress. These were networks of people who believed in something more for their lives, and our global community. This was work that could be financially rewarding and meaningful. I wanted all of these things but couldn't access them without first letting my weird flag out for myself to see and, in return, for all the weirdos to see too.

Over the years, I've had friends question my actions as a mother. Stating that their mom never did such things like drive them to exams because their anxiety was causing them to freeze, help map out course selection, or meet with advisors to discuss learning accommodations at college, to which I would respond, "Why should your mum be my benchmark?" It fueled me to do the best I could do on any given day. To my delight, I found myself surrounded by people that had my back and were on "our team". There were child psychologists, educators, and support teachers who became friends and were my cheerleaders, genuinely wanting my children to soar!

As a family, we found our ability to embrace our weird, and to be our complete selves together at all times. We aren't perfect. We are weird and we are different, and to me, that is perfect. So when my kids come up to me and tell me that someone called them "weird", I look at them, smile, and tell them about how amazing it is to be weird because truthfully weird, by definition, is just describing something that you don't know how to feel about yet. There's absolutely nothing wrong with that. I encourage them to be themselves, to be authentic and true to how they want to show up in this world. Isn't that what we all crave?

Life is a series of weird events strung together, and if you're lucky enough, your kids will only validate how beautiful it is to shine your true self, no matter how weird it seems to others. All my kids are embarking on their own journey of life, and I will do anything for them because they're dope, funny and most of all WEIRD.

The moral of the story is, be your authentic self while standing in your truth and coming from a place of love. Stay strong in your convictions and your sense of self, and laugh. Laugh often. I think I'm funny. Hilarious, even! Because I let myself. In a sea of hundreds of birds, I'll find the one with the peg leg. I've decided that is a gift: to see the one who was weird and unique, find it interesting, and give it attention for being okay with standing out. Life is too short to try to be normal to make other people accept us comfortably, on their terms. Stay weird, my friends.

Acknowledgements: Much love to my famjam for always being in my corner, and a HUGE shout- out of thanks to Sarah Swain, Olivia Shwetz and Cassie Jeans for their guidance and unwavering support.

About the Author

Barbara McBryer lives with her husband, three children and crazy Goldendoodle in beautiful British Columbia. She is passionate about supporting and advocating for her children, and helping them to find their own voices. She is an information junkie, wanting to learn all of the things and is always up for a challenge, no matter how seemingly difficult. An avid home cook, she enjoys researching new recipes to try, using her unsuspecting husband as tester. Barbara is infamous for her facial expressions, animated storytelling (likely with dramatic flair), and is known to laugh out loud obnoxiously in movie theatres. She encourages everyone to embrace their weird side. For real, what is normal any-way?

IG: @hashtagalltheweirdos

FB:@barbara.mcbryer

CREATIVITY

Creativity knows no lines and no boundaries. It ebbs and it flows with full permission to change course at any given moment. Creativity is a world where everything is possible, yet nothing is the same. It is sparked by both joy and sadness alike. Inspired by love and by pain. It is freeing, healing and both maddening and exciting. The art of creating exists within all of us, and we can surprise ourselves with our own unique and beautiful abilities we have unknowingly kept locked in the vault.

Patricia's story is of a beautiful birth that came after a tragic loss. In grief, we are allowed to experience joy, just like any other. A lost soul is always able to find her way home, and creativity was the navigation system that allowed Patricia to continue on her life's journey through the confusion of love and heartache.

GETTING MY 'HAPPY' ON

"The culture was in the 'agriculture' and Art was the man who ran the grain elevator."

Patricia Coulter

CHAPTER TEN

Getting My Happy On

I will come clean now. I was addicted from the start! There was something about it that kept calling me back. I couldn't stop! I would lie awake at night, dreaming, planning, preparing for my next time. My drug of choice was not what one would think. I became madly in love with painting. Each time the lush colour began flowing down the canvas, I was mesmerized. The energy, the vibrancy, the boost that came from the paint was exhilarating! It was as if I was opening up an energy field, one that spoke of warmth, tranquility, and positive energy. Time slipped away, the outside world was silenced, my task list momentarily suspended.

Coming to this style of painting is part of my personal journey. When my youngest daughter was killed by a drunk driver, I fell into a dark place. It was as if I had been walking along a frozen lake and suddenly fell through the ice, plunging downwards further each day. I knew I could swim up toward the light, but it was a struggle. I had days in which I thought, "What is the point? What is the point of anything?" I was fortunate in that I had a supportive spouse and family network, a demanding job, and thoughtful friends who often phoned me and said, "We're going for a walk" or "We're going to yoga at seven! I'm picking you up!" Knowing I had to move ahead, one foot at a time, I remembered how my daughter and I had painted together, usually on Sunday afternoons at the kitchen table. We used the book "The Readers' Digest Complete Guide to Art" as our reference. We liked the watercolour painting section the best. Using a simple set of watercolour paints and brushes, we loved creating! As I wrestled with my heartache, I recalled how much fun that was and got out my paint set. At first, my paintings were very small and very dark. Gradually, I began to notice how time had slipped away and how much better I felt. I began painting more, painting larger, using brighter hues. I especially loved the wet-on-wet technique, where the watercolours blended, flowed, merged, and hung out together. Searching for brighter hues and wanting to work in a larger format led me to discover fluid acrylic paint. When I began experimenting with pieces of canvas so that the paint could flow into organic shapes, I was in love. The colours were breathtaking, the shapes organic, and the energy flowing. Often, when I am painting, I can feel my daughter's presence. Sometimes she is looking down and smiling, and other times she is saying, "Stop right there!"

As a teacher, I had gradually morphed from being a high school English teacher to an art teacher. I knew firsthand how art could be a form of therapy for students. The act of mark making acts as a soothing balm to ragged souls. I was amazed at how painting had uplifted me, and I was eager to pass it onto others who were experiencing pain or troubles of sorts.

I wasn't raised in a particularly artsy household. My parents were both farmers who worked very hard to make a go of it. My father loved to tinker with machines and often made many adjustments before taking some equipment out to the field. My mother was a homemaker who incorporated many creative acts into her daily life. To her, a recipe was just a starting place and she added and subtracted items using ingredients she had on hand. She created many unique garments, using ideas from the weekly farm publication The Western Producer. Also, I think she understood the value of play for children and wasn't worried about a mess. In our rural setting, we didn't go to concerts or art galleries. The culture was in the "agriculture", and Art was the man who ran the grain elevator.

When my parents were moving out of their old farmhouse, they were clearing out the attic. They found a drawing I had done as a five-year-old. I had drawn the whole yard with farmhouse, barn, and granaries. My dad was driving the tractor and my Mom was hanging clothes on the line. The family dog was in there too! Because there wasn't a kindergarten program for rural children at that time, a readiness test was given. Part of the test was to draw a picture. The examiner had written on the back of my drawing, "This child is very creative and should be given every opportunity to develop her talents." I think my parents went home happy and went on with their busy lives. I knew growing up that I loved to create, to make things. I experimented with many mediums and methods. I tried sewing, quilting, and working with glass. It was as if I had the personal philosophy of leaving no stone unturned as I experimented with my creative journey. So when I discovered that I could layer paint onto canvas, I was hooked! I knew I had found my thing! What I had loved as a child, had patiently waited for me! Even though I hadn't had any art training as a child, this love of creating hadn't left me. It was lying dormant, just waiting for me to rediscover it. The blend of colours, the flow of organic shapes, the way to speak and tell my own story, it was all just waiting to be rekindled.

I have had amazing success with my paintings. I was chosen to go to shows like the Art Expo in New York, New York and Art Basel week in Miami, Florida. I was featured at the Canadian celebration for the Canada 150 celebrations at the Westin Hotel in Singapore in April 2017. I have been featured in the PBS documentary, Put Some Colour In Your Life, with host Graeme Stevenson; this allowed me to meet fans and viewers from all over the globe. And I was thrilled to see my painting, "Brimming", on the cover of Art Business magazine.

Throughout my creative journey, I began to notice that no matter where I went in the world, people said the same thing. "Oh, I'm just not creative!" I want to grab them and say that 'Yes, yes, you are creative!" I want to tell everyone that their creativity is just waiting for them. There is a small pilot light of creativity burning within each one of us, but most fear that the heavy work boot of jobs, relationships, etc. has stomped out their creative flame.

The first thing one has to do is become quiet and still. Stillness is required for that small voice of creativity to speak to us. With our ever increasing barrage of social media, we are bombarded with things to do and people to see. We have to consciously make time in our busy day to just sit, sit quietly, and let the worries of the world slip away, if only for a few minutes. If we spend all of our alone time on social media, we may not be giving ourselves the chance to be the person we were meant to be. Getting away from the endless racket of social media helps us to listen to that small, quiet voice inside us.

Think back to when you were young, around the ages of seven to ten. What did you like to do when you were on your own? Use those early interests as a starting place to find creativity in your life now. Maybe you liked to write in your journal, that one with the little lock on it, and that leads you to journaling, and maybe that leads to blogging. Maybe you remember writing poems in school and that leads you to writing poetry, which leads you to writing songs or short stories. Remember the fun you had in band class? One could dig out their clarinet from the back of the closet and start playing again. One realizes they like music and they start singing in a choir, and that leads to playing in a handbell choir. One's path to recovering their creative story probably won't be a direct, straight line, but rather a curvy, winding road that gradually steers one in the right direction.

Now, think of something you like to work with. There will be one sensory detail that appeals more strongly to your senses. When the abstract artist Willem de Kooning emigrated to America, he worked as a house painter. When asked if that wasn't related to his art, he said, "I like paint". Maybe the texture of wool will have a special appeal and that could lead one to knitting, crocheting, weaving, or other needle arts. The porous feeling of clay may bring about an interest in pottery. Perhaps one is attracted to the flow of black ink across a crisp white page, and that leads to an interest in calligraphy, or pen and ink drawings. Maybe you find yourself wrapping your hands around a wooden bowl and that leads to woodworking!

Another way to find our special creative powers is to think of something one does where time disappears. Something where one loses all track of time and looks up, amazed at how much time has passed. Wander around a large bookstore and see what calls out to you. People have often said a book fell off of the shelf right in front of them, and picking it up and briefly reading the cover led to a new interest.

A few hours at an art gallery, trade show or museum show can be a powerful indicator of where one's creativity may be waiting. What item was most powerful to you? If you had to tell someone about the one thing you recalled the most, what is the underlying message there? What really piqued your interest when you were travelling?

So often, we pride ourselves on being busy. When you're chatting with someone and they ask how you are, do you say, "I've been so busy"? Does being busy make us feel good about ourselves? Do we wear busyness as a badge of courage? Is being busy keeping us from doing some soul searching, facing the truth about a negative situation, or are we being fearful of what might emerge when we're not dashing madly from here to there. Creativity needs quiet in order for us to hear it above the hub.

The writer, Anne Lamont, in her book Bird By Bird, advises people to be open to the start of any creative project and know that it's not going to be great. She calls them SFD - Shitty First Drafts! The main thing is that you have started. Make mistakes, make big mistakes, make glorious mistakes, you're learning. It's only going to get better. Set yourself up for success. If you've had too much Netflix and not enough Bowflex, find ways to make exercise a part of your day. Have your workout outfit ready to go and have a buddy who keeps you going. Something that worked for me was to have a small paint set, paper and brushes on the kitchen counter. Whenever I had a few minutes, I sketched or painted. I knew they weren't going to be masterpieces but it was a relaxing way to fill in time. I found having a small painting set in my vehicle was helpful for times when I had to wait. When my car wasn't ready when the service department said it was going to be, I was quite happy to draw a picture or doodle out a design.

Set yourself a challenge. Many artists challenge themselves with goals of doing 30 paintings in 30 days, 100 paintings in 100 days, etc. They all reported how much improved their skills became and how they found they could work their creativity in all sorts of variable conditions. Comedian Jerry Seinfeld swears by putting a checkmark on a big calendar page. You will find that you don't want to stop the momentum. Big red checkmarks, gold stars, a punch card, it all works! A simple tool that makes for powerful results.

Writing in a gratitude journal has been a powerful tool for me. Being grateful changes our thinking from a "woe is me" mindset to being thankful for the wonderful lives we lead. My gratitude journal gives me pages of documentation to remind me what I am thankful for, and acts as a guide for my future. An attitude of gratitude brings opportunities. It shows the universe what you are thankful for, and sends you more of that good stuff.

The whole concept of art as a career is often discouraged in favor of getting a "real" job. Once a monetary value is attached to creativity, the whole creative process can be shut down. Shy away from the urge to share your creativity projects with others, especially at the beginning. As soon as someone sees the beginning of a painting, people often say "Are you going to be rich and famous?" You will be tempted to say, "Probably not!" Our first few tries at being creative can be intimidating when it doesn't turn out like you had envisioned. Better answers are, "Maybe" or "Yes, but just not yet!" We have to be open to letting things unfold, simmer, and percolate. It was a basic need, an itch, a want to create. By being open to possibilities and closing off the naysayers, our creative voices get a chance to speak. Your creative voice has been stifled for so long, it needs time and practice to get rolling. Blowing out your comfort zone can be life changing. Don't feel you have to commit to the rest of your life. Take your new interests for a test drive. Try it for a while before you decide.

We tend to think of "basic needs" in terms of bare bones survival, food and shelter, but our need for creating is just as foundational to our well-being. We want to know and understand, we want to love and experience belonging. We want to manipulate the stuff of the world with our hands and our minds as a way of making meaning, learning who we are and what we can do. As adults, we have often cut ourselves off from these drives. We have to give ourselves permission to create, to let go, to fail and get back up! Creativity has held out an invisible hand to me and lifted me up in many ways. For anyone struggling with grief or in a stressful situation, look for the soothing balm of creativity. So stop waiting for the conditions to be perfect. You will wait a long time, a very long time. Instead of postponing your path, make do with where you are now. Just start. Be open to what happens. Start again. The benefits of doing something creative will help you get your happy on, and possibly even help you regain some lost health. Being creative lets a warm wave of well-being wash over you. The world is waiting for you!

Acknowledgements: First and foremost, thank you to our editor, Sarah Swain. Despite many hurdles to overcome, you have been supportive of my progress as an artist and a writer. I am sure you had challenging days but you always kept a positive mindset and gentle guidance. The quotation that Hillary Clinton made famous, "It takes a village to raise a child", applies to me. I'm grateful to my extraordinary team who help me in innumerable ways, my husband Larry, my daughters Laura and Erin, and that whole village of thoughtful and kind supporters who all take turns with the heavy lifting of nurturing an artist.

About the Author

After retiring from teaching high school art, Patricia Coulter is thankful to be able to devote her time to developing and advancing her art career. Along with teaching painting on cruise ships such as the Queen Mary 2 and the Celebrity Infinity ships, she also teaches an online course. Patricia has received many awards for her art and is the only Canadian to receive the Staedtler-Mars Award twice. Her paintings have been included in five recently-published books: Acrylics Unleashed, Incite 2, Acrylic Works; Celebrating Texture, and others. Her paintings have been featured in solo and group shows in galleries in Canada, the United States and Singapore.

Patricia was thrilled to be one of the artists filmed in 2016 for the series, Put Some Colour In Your Life, with host Graeme Stevenson. This series is shown on PBS stations and on YouTube. Her painting, "Blue Rhapsody", was an honorable mention in the Manhattan Arts online gallery for the exhibition, New Beginnings. Her painting, "Brimming", was featured on the cover of Art Business News, and she was selected as one of the Top Artists to Watch by Art Business and Redwood Media. In March 2016, she was honoured to receive the Woman of Influence Overall Winner Award by the Cold Lake Women of Influence Committee. Patricia was honoured to be a featured artist at the Canada 150 Celebrations in Singapore in 2017. Her goal is to bring joy to others through art, either through her paintings or by encouraging others to find their own joy in their creative endeavours.

www.patriciacoulter.com

IG: @patriciacoulterart

GROWTH

Growth comes with pain, and with pain comes more growth. When we have one, we will likely experience the other. It's mental. It's intellectual. It's spiritual. It's emotional. And with each new growth spurt comes another dose of pain. The pain of realizing we are the only thing standing in our way can often feel like too much responsibility to bear. It seems impossible to think we could ever find ourselves in a situation we would have never dreamed for ourselves. To recognize that behaviour repeating itself over and over again can leave us feeling either defeated and ashamed that we allowed it to happen, or motivated and empowered because we recognize our own power to change course.

Rose's story is one of radical ownership of her own evolution through some of the most extreme life circumstances that most would never experience in a lifetime. Rose shares her journey of quadriplegia, insecurities, breast implant illness and the freefall into a state of surrender that would spark her journey of growth into the woman she is today.

CHECK YOURSELF BEFORE YOU WRECK YOURSELF

"What doesn't kill you, makes you conscious"

−Rose Finlay

CHAPTER ELEVEN

Check Yourself Before You Wreck Yourself

It's the middle of February. It's a winter that has overall, been relatively mild. The ground is frozen, the trees are quiet and the deadening silence of life is getting a little underwhelming. Dark, cold winters are hard for many people but especially so when your wheels are your superpower. You see, while they're definitely what sets me apart from the rest, they also keep me stranded in the snow. Suffering a cervical spinal cord injury as a teen was incredibly traumatic. It took me almost 12 years to really grasp and understand just how many positive things were a result of something so catastrophic. I couldn't fathom something that took so much from me having a positive impact in any way.

My disability, however, wasn't my most difficult challenge or struggle. My toxic thoughts were. My deprecated self-worth from growing up with a narcissistic father kept me begging for love in all the wrong places and very much in the victim mindset. For the first ten years of my adult life I decided that remaining in relationships that were detrimental to my self-esteem was somehow better than struggling with the physical challenges of a disabled life. I continually settled for less because I didn't ever feel like I deserved more. I did, though. We all do. We deserve a love free from the chains of judgement and expectations. We deserve a love that both encourages and inspires growth and personal development. We must first learn to give that love to ourselves. The phrase "in order to love another, you must first love yourself" has always seemed so cliché to me. I knew that I was capable of loving another so much that my self-worth came second. What's more selfless than that? What I didn't know was that by putting my self-worth second, I was diminishing my own power. I was essentially giving my power away. I was constantly feeling inexplicably insecure and anxious. I tried so hard to just be invisible to the world.

It wasn't until I realized that I was living completely out of alignment with who I was and my purpose here in this life, that these behaviours and thought patterns began to shift. I'm not supposed to be invisible! I was gifted this life and countless opportunities for a reason. I had so much to share with the world around me but instead I found myself hiding in fear. I ignored all the warning signs that were trying to guide me back to my path. I thought it was normal to numb the pain in my marriage with prescription medication. I thought it was normal to recluse from my close friends when I couldn't tell them all the things that were going on in my life. I thought this overwhelming feeling of anxiousness and lack of self-worth was normal because that was all I saw around me. I hadn't created an environment for myself that allowed me to see or believe anything different. I thought staying in these situations was better than facing my fears. Fear kept me chained. I was so determined to show the people around me that I could make it work and make the best out of what I had been handed, rather than shedding it all and choosing something new. Something better for myself. I was chained to my past because I was so committed to my mistakes.

The inexplicable, uncontrollable anxiety started after the birth of my second son. My first child with my third husband. I know, I know... There was a significant decline in our marriage after only a year together. I couldn't understand why the patterns in my marriages kept repeating themselves. Insecurity, infidelity and control. I blamed them. How could someone else's infidelity be at all my fault? The lesson here was not fault but rather that I didn't have enough self-respect to set boundaries that allowed me to walk away from relationships that were suffocating, draining and hurting me. At the time, I couldn't see how my own beliefs about what I deserved in life were attracting these relationships both romantically and socially. I was welcoming them in and allowing them to stay by not setting clear boundaries.

In June of 2017, I made the very decision that changed my course. I decided that breast implants were the solution to both my marital problems and my self-worth issues. I thought that maybe, just maybe, if I became more physically attractive to my husband, I would have a newfound sense of confidence. My mind told me that my confidence was directly linked to the success and stability of my family, but my soul was telling me otherwise. I remember feeling uneasy about the decision, but the medications coursing through my body made it easy to ignore. I went through with the surgery.

Post-surgery, my reality came into focus very quickly and very clearly. My body began to fail as BII (Breast Implant Illness) consumed me. I remember feeling like a complete failure. First and foremost, as a mother. My children felt my fear and they watched as I deteriorated. I was, again, so committed to my mistakes that I didn't agree to remove the implants for eight months, even with them draining my health right before my eyes.

The realizations weren't all at once. They came slowly, as my symptoms changed and fluctuated. I began to listen to exactly what my body was telling me. Each symptom brought a new lesson and challenged my commitment to this life. Pain teaches you, if you listen. Emotional or physical. Emotions, in general, are the soul's way of communicating. My emotional pain had been telling me for years that I was not fulfilling my purpose and living my passion. I wasn't choosing myself. I chose to let my fears override this communication and instead, I blocked it out with prescription medications and dangerous cosmetic surgery, something that many women have done over the years because we fear being labeled as crazy, unstable, ugly or different. It has sadly become more acceptable to just ignore these insecurities than allow people to openly heal their wounds in a safe environment. We have a mounting mental health crisis in North America because we have continuously tried to make people, women in particular, fit into boxes rather than express their creative freedom.

There was no override for the physical illnesses that manifested in my life. There was no longer a quick fix or pill that I could pop to make it all better, or go away. I simply got to the point where I had experienced too much poison - mind, body and soul - and I had to begin to detox every area immediately, if I wanted to continue in this life. Rock bottom was realizing that all the behaviours that I learned as a child, my survival skills, had led me to this place. Realizing that my survival was now dependent upon deprogramming this social conditioning was both empowering and daunting. How was I supposed to let go of all the things I used as armour? How was vulnerability, that I previously feared so much and saw as a weakness, going to save me? I had to bare all the things about myself that I kept in secret, instead of hiding them in fear. I had to trust that my soul innately knew what I needed. Surrender. I remember hearing this word as I meditated. Surrender control, surrender expectations, surrender it all and just be. That thought in and of itself was inconceivable to me. I was the captain of this ship! Control! Control was what I lived by! It's how I managed my disability, my relationships, everything! I couldn't control my body, so I made every attempt at controlling everything around me in a desperate attempt to keep my fears and insecurities at bay. How could I just give that up, and surrender to what was?

This journey brought with it a spiritual connection to Source that I had otherwise believed to be "some hokey stuff that religious people bought into". I didn't exactly grow up with a solid religious belief system, even though I went to Catholic school most of my elementary years. What I didn't realize about this divine connection, was that it was truly about becoming connected to myself. Loving myself. Embracing myself. Accepting myself. Trusting myself. Trust was something that I had struggled with for years because I chose to hold onto betrayal instead. I chose not to trust so as not to be naive, because I defined naivety as weakness. I had no compassion for myself and so I held onto each painful experience, like I insisted on it. These were my survival skills. These were the things that I thought were protecting me from heartache. My own behaviours were the cause of my pain.

Letting go of control, gave me back my power. Learning to trust my intuition fiercely, gave me back my light. As I moved through these transitions, my surroundings began to change and my overall health started to improve. I'm still navigating the unknowns of breast implant illness and silicone toxicity but each day, I feel my light becoming brighter, and less toxic in every possible way. I have had to face some seriously painful truths. I not only had to learn on more than one occasion, how to live with complicated physical challenges, I had to learn to love myself even while at my lowest points. The way we love ourselves shows others how we need to be loved. Ah-ha! In order to attract the love I desired and deserved, I first had to give it to myself. Even without boobs. Even while my body was malnourished. Even when I felt abandoned. Even when I felt betrayed. Even when I felt afraid. Even when I felt insecure. Even when I didn't feel good enough. I had to love myself through it all.

Growth is painful, but also necessary and completely worth it. I felt like I was losing far more often than I was winning, and therefore something needed to change. With nowhere else to go, and no one else to turn to, I had no choice but to turn to me. Returning to old habits, or tucking away in hiding when things got tough were no longer solutions I could accept. My health was fragile, and yet my soul was screaming for me to be strong. Being independent was something I took great pride in, but being independent to the point of not allowing myself to soften and accept any help was continuing to make my situation direr. Changing these behaviours, and allowing myself to receive help and genuine care and concern from others was an entire life transition all on its own. Sabotaging my own growth and evolution by pushing people away and shutting down only caused the emotions stirring within me to have nowhere else to reside but my body, which had been through enough already.

Self-mastery has been an amazing tool for healing, because now I know when to reach out before hitting these low points. I have a newfound sense of self-awareness and can detect when my mindset may be starting to decline, and nip it in the bud before I fall too deeply. Falling back into alignment with myself gifted me with the ability to discover my passion and purpose that had been kept hidden beneath so many cold, hard layers for so long. And stepping into this newfound zest for living has attracted an entirely new network of people who I desire to spend my time with and learn from. My soul tribe are the people who see me for me, and know how to help get me through the hard days. For someone who used to be somewhat of a recluse, learning the art of vulnerability and transparency was my missing link. In order for new people to enter my life, I had to allow for myself to be seen in ways I had never done before. Opening up and showing my flaws to the world has been one of the more transformational things I have done. I had to learn to show up for myself instead of letting the actions of others derail my mind and ultimately my life. I had to fully grasp just how much the Universe had in store for me, as there was so much more that I was being called to do. My own personal journey through physical health adversity provided me with an incredible opportunity to help other women heal, and better yet avoid serious health issues by not listening to the subtle cues of the mind, body and soul. For this I'm eternally grateful.

My disability and BII do not dictate my life, though many people think they would. Sure, it can be a lot to manage some days, but suffering is subjective. Everyone's capacity for handling crisis is different. We are a culture shrouded in shame, and we simply can't afford to make it any harder on ourselves by allowing fear to have far more control than it ever should. It's time we speak up and question all of this social conditioning that leads us to think we aren't good enough in the first place. It's time we start asking ourselves the hard questions. Why are we judging ourselves and others so harshly? Why are we forcing ourselves to be unhappy in order to conform to someone else's expectation of us? I was recently asked by a family member if my tribulations would encourage me to keep my guard up. My answer was, "No, absolutely not". I chose to forgive others and forgive myself. I chose to release the pain. I chose to have compassion for myself for not knowing better, sooner. I chose to no longer wear my trauma like a mask, and shed the identity of being a victim of life. The anger just simply needed to go, and knowing that anger is no longer the emotion in charge reassures me every day that I am, in fact, healing.

If there's anything that I have learned about my personal life through the help of mentors and coaches, is that everyone's trauma is different, and therefore so is their healing. What connects us all together, is that healing is a universally messy business, no matter how we choose to move through it. The path is not linear. It's up and down, two steps forward and three backwards. Amazing days and horrible days. But it is possible, and it is on us to own it.

"It does not matter how slowly you go,
as long as you do not stop"
- Confucius

Sometimes we aren't given a choice about things in our life and we are met with unforeseen circumstances ranging from minor to catastrophic. I have experienced a spectrum of anything from heartbreak to being told I would never walk again, to being informed that my attempt at self-love in the form of silicon bags was actual-ly poisoning me from the inside out. Regardless of what happens, whether expected or not, our commitment to our own growth must remain consistent. There are things that are in our control in this lifetime and there are many things that are not. Sometimes the game changes halfway through. We still have something on our side though, every single time: choice. We can re-group and respond in a way that empowers us, or we can let it be our demise. That choice is always ours to make. That is where we begin to take back our power. That is self-mastery. If we don't choose growth, we are wasting our finite time here in this form. We could have been focusing our energy on becoming even just a slightly better version of ourselves than we were yester-day, and encouraging those around us to do the same. Sometimes leading by example is the best way to in-spire and motivate others. Regardless, I have learned firsthand that change starts within. The human experi-ence is a strange and beautiful thing. Learn to connect, to love, to listen to it all.

Acknowledgements: This step into authoring has been a very long time in the making. I used to always joke with my friends and family that I would write books once I retired because I was too busy living my life to spend time writing about it. I guess with illness and recovery downtime, this time came a little sooner. If my retirement looks anything like this "downtime", I'm going to be an incredibly busy woman until my last breath. Who knew that writing a chapter about transparency and vulnerability would make my commitment to my own growth that much more solid? With that though comes a lot of gratitude for the people who have loved and supported me through this crazy transition. Firstly, my babies. Although they're too young yet to really understand it all, they're my "why". Ryker, Keltonn and Lachlan, I am so proud to be your Mom. I love you all "too much". To my family, thank you for continuing to support me and believe in me - even when you don't always understand me. To my soul tribe, thank you for holding space, encouraging my growth and loving me hard. Lastly, thank you to The Great Canadian Woman for everything you stand for and the incredible sense of belonging you give to women supporting each other.

About the Author

After sustaining a high level cervical spinal cord injury at the tender age of 17, Rose Finlay quickly became acquainted with overcoming struggle and adversity. Her unstoppable spirit and ferociously positive outlook pushed her to chase her lifelong goals of motherhood and entrepreneurship, despite being a quadriplegic. Holistic health coaching and empowerment mentoring have given Rose purpose and kept her driven and committed to her own personal growth and development. Her interest in natural wellness and alternative medicine sparked her passion for holistic healing and eventually lead to her spiritual journey into quantum health. Rose found her power and personal freedom when she finally allowed herself to step into her truth, and take full ownership of her individuality. This resilience and perseverance were two of the qualities that helped her survive and push through a terrifying, life threatening illness caused by her breast implants.

This free-spirited, single mom is now focused on raising her three little men while striving to be a consistent example of gratitude and empathy. She is smashing all stereotypes and continuing to push the limitations placed on her by societal skepticism. This shining light pours inspiration into all the cracks in your soul whilst evoking a strong belief in self. Prepare to shift from survive to thrive.

www.essentiallyrose.com

IG: @essentially.rose.hhmc

TRUST

Trust gifts us with the ability to make decisions when the decisions before us feel like too much to bear. Like choosing between hard and harder, between fear and terror, or between love and passion. The options before us feel impossible. We feel like we need a sign, or we need more information, or we need to think more or learn more, or await the validation of others before we proceed. Yet when we search for the answers outside of ourselves, we steal our own power away. Our only true option becomes to drop into a deep sense of trust, that can only come from within.

Olivia's story highlights the importance of knowing that our own intuition is enough. Our decisions don't need to make sense to anyone other than ourselves, especially when it seems like no matter what we do, it won't be easy. It's a story of deep love, deep sadness and knee buckling fear, coupled with a powerful inner knowing that we are supported in all that we choose, when we choose from our own heart space.

SILVER LININGS

"Love can hit you like a tsunami wave.
It comes at you out of nowhere, it rises to heights you
never anticipated and in the end it crashes - destroying
everything in its wake."

—Olivia Shwetz

CHAPTER TWELVE

Silver Linings

In 2013, I lost someone I loved very dearly. As much as he will always be a part of me, there's a bigger part to our story that hasn't been shared. His life, and his past aren't mine to share, but there is a part of our time together that can no longer be locked away. It's been eating away at me for too many years, and I know how poisonous this part of my life has been on me. I've been given a divine opportunity to bring it all to light, and I'll be damned if I let it continue to rip me apart inside.

We came from different worlds, but were able to meet each other on neutral ground. He came from a history of living fast and free, born in beautiful British Columbia and growing up in the Kootenays. He didn't abide or listen to much of what anyone else said. He lived his life on his own terms, and I admired him for that. Myself, I was tied to the rules and guidelines of society. Born and raised in the pridelands of Alberta, I was someone who never stepped too far out of line before course-correcting and apologizing for taking up space. There were definitely times when I thought I was in over my head, but his lifestyle was so different compared to what I'd experienced, that my curiosity took the lead. I was drawn to him like a moth to a flame.

Shortly into our relationship, only four weeks, I found out I was pregnant! It came as a complete shock! Part of me had always envisioned the moment I found out I was pregnant to be one that filled me with joy, excitement and a wave of love I'd never experienced before - this wasn't that at all. Instead I was filled with fear, uncertainty and dread. How had I been so careless? How had I let this happen with a man I hardly even knew? What was I going to do? The questions raced through my mind as I blamed myself for what I was experiencing, all the while holding the positive pregnancy test in my shaking hands, as I sat on the front porch of my townhome alone, and turned into a mess of sobs and tears.

My support system during this phase of my life was the polar opposite of what I have now. I felt incredibly alone, vulnerable and had no confidence in opening up to the few people I had in my life. I didn't want to turn to my family, I'd put them through enough over the last few years. I didn't want to open up to the few friends I did have, out of fear of judgement. Most importantly I had no idea how to let the new man in my life in on the fact that I was now pregnant with his child. Completely helpless and alone, I didn't have the slightest idea of how he would react to this major life-altering situation in which we now found ourselves. My instincts urged me to start to look at our options. I decided to wait a week to tell him, when he was back from his shift up north in Fort McMurray, where he worked as a linesman.

Preparing for the worst, I took the lead and booked myself in to see my doctor to confirm everything. Something I never thought I would find myself doing at the age of twenty-four was booking in for an abortion. My heart sank into my chest as I Googled "abortion clinic, Edmonton". Had it really come to this? Was I being sensible? Should I call someone? Who? We've only just met, I didn't even know if he WANTED kids, let alone if we were a good match to become parents together! I'd seen how these kinds of situations had a tendency to play out. There was a small possibility we'd be one of the few who make it work and live happily ever after. Yet somewhere deep down I felt like there was a higher chance of me ending up a single parent who resents my child's father. Booking the abortion appointment was one of the hardest things I'd ever had to do in my life. I remember the awful feelings of guilt and shame that bubbled up in me as I booked in. Part of me didn't even believe I was actually pregnant as I placed my hand on my stomach, knowing there was new life being created inside, even though I didn't feel a single thing. To help me cope I turned to the one thing I could trust, writing. I started a new journal where I began writing to my possible future child. Sharing my fears and apprehensions about this journey we were about to go on together, unsure if would be weeks or years that we'd share. I'd pour my heart out about the fears I had of becoming a mom, with a man I hardly knew. That he seemed pretty incredible so far, so maybe there was a chance? There was a glimmer of hope that there was a happy ending in this somewhere.

He came home a week later, and I opened up to him about the pregnancy. Taken aback at first, he was still level-headed about the whole thing, positive even. So positive that I called the next day and cancelled the appointment at the abortion clinic. For a couple of weeks, things were great. He was moving into my place, we were buying a truck with an extended cab, and beginning to share the news of our miraculous conception with our family and friends. For a brief time, I thought for sure we were going to be "one of the few" who figured it all out, despite the lackluster enthusiasm from family and friends. I was not the best at sharing exciting news back then, and would just awkwardly drop, "Oh and I'm pregnant" in random conversation. It didn't matter, did it, that I was almost robotic about it? I felt we could make something special out of this, that we could really make it all work, but I was still struggling that this was reality. Then, as suddenly as those feelings appeared, they were washed away and things began to take a turn for the worse.

It was over a period of four short weeks that everything went from fairytale to nightmare. What do you expect when you've only known someone for a few weeks? There are bound to be a few learning curves, right? A few bumps in the road are to be expected. Well, those learning curves for me were finding a way to understand his mental health issues, and problems with addiction. These were things I had never encountered before, but I wasn't afraid to support him. His mental health quickly began to decline and he started doubting the baby was even his. His mental health was so out of focus that I found myself being placed in dangerous situations that no one should be in, especially when pregnant. Something had to give.

Knowing I couldn't help him and take proper care of myself to bring a healthy baby into the world, I came to terms with the decision that needed to be made. I had to decide if I wanted to do this alone, or even do it at all. I knew I was running out of time to go through with an abortion, so I had to act fast. It was then I found the same feelings of fear and guilt rising up as I made another appointment with the clinic. I wouldn't be canceling this one. In my heart I knew that if we were meant to be together, we could try again when he was healthy, and back to being the man I met just a few short weeks ago. I saw the light in him, and knew he had good inside that was trying to stay visible. He was being buried by the weight of his mental health issues. He'd confided in me that he was never meant to see his 30th birthday during all this. I truly loved him with my whole being, and wanted to be the one to throw him one hell of a 30th birthday bash! I wanted to be the one who saved him. Love can hit you like a tsunami wave. It comes at you out of nowhere, it rises to heights you never anticipated and in the end it crashes - destroying everything in its wake.

We didn't speak a word the morning of the appointment. We drove to the city in silence. We sat in the waiting room in silence. Then, when the nurses confirmed how far along I was, tossing any questions of doubt that it wasn't his out the window, the silence spoke for him. That's when the nurse handed me the medication to begin the process. There would be no turning back once that step was done. I looked at him, hoping he'd grab me and we'd run for the high hills out of there. The silence hung in the room like a heavy fog, which only confirmed for me that we both were not ready for this. So I courageously and terrifyingly took the next step. There's nothing quite like sitting in a room with other women, all there for the same reason, all filled with guilt, uncertainty, doubt and shame. That kind of silence is deafening. Sitting in that waiting room, staring at the floor felt like hours. Part of me wanted to run, but the process had already begun. So I put on the bravest face I had as they called my name to go next, like getting vaccinations as a kid at school. As I think back on this moment now, I remember a nurse, who I wish I could thank, because the words she whispered into my ear, though faded now, as the procedure was completed were an important part of my healing process. I say this because as everything was happening I kept thinking that things shouldn't be this quiet. This is too soon. I should be hearing cries of a new life beginning, not the silence as my unborn baby's life ending. She'll never know how much her words meant to me, and helped me to cope with the extremely difficult decision I made that day.

The guilt and the shame one feels for making that difficult decision are impossible to explain. The journal I'd started writing in to my unborn baby, only made things worse now. So in the first few days after having the procedure, I tore the pages out and burned them. I then had to lie to my family, friends and everyone about the decision we made. I couldn't own up to what I, we, had decided to do. So I lied to them all, saying I'd had a miscarriage. I thought that would make it easier; it didn't. Keeping it a secret, and trying to hide it away, fed my soul a poison for which the only antidote was a mix of ownership and honesty. The choice to be dishonest would bite me several times over the coming years before I could formulate the antidote. Each time I'd lie about it, I'd rip the scab off the somewhat healed part of my soul for the choice made.

The months after the abortion things only picked up speed, and took on a rather rollercoaster-like motion. They were filled with ups and downs, good days and bad days. I was trying to heal physically and mentally, and also trying to get him back on the bright side of life. He was trying to get back to work and get his mental health back in order, but the system was failing us. He'd spend some time in hospitals, and speaking with doctors, but in the end, his heart just couldn't take it anymore. He would leave this physical world only a few months after we made the choice to end the pregnancy, and only a couple of days before what would have been our first Valentine's Day. Now I was alone. No man. No longer pregnant. Not at all where I thought I was heading just seven short months ago. I'd spend Valentine's Day with his family, helping them plan a funeral for their 29-year-old son, a man I'd loved fiercely for only a short time, but what felt like a lifetime.

There's a small part of me that wishes we'd never met, only because of the tragedy that would ensue in our short time together. I know better though, meeting him was a necessary catalyst for my exponential growth and in my heart of hearts, I also realize I was put on his path to be beside him in his final moments.

It wasn't easy for me, grief is an enigma, and everyone experiences it differently. There were countless nights I would lie awake and wonder how things may have been different had I decided to keep the baby. The scenarios that played out in my head were enough to drive someone mad. Maybe he wouldn't have died? Maybe I could have changed things? Maybe, maybe, maybe! Everything that happened, had to happen. Tragedy is a fact of life, death is a fact of life, and sometimes if we look hard enough, we can see the silver lining hidden within the most difficult of tragedies.

Fast forward to 2019, and I've found my silver lining! I have been able to heal my body, mind and soul. All of this because I chose a new direction for my life after losing him, and aborting the pregnancy. Through it all I've also welcomed an incredible man into my life, at first as a friend and then as one of the most amazing men I've given my heart to. The world works in mysterious ways you see, I know that we were brought together in divine time. While I was struggling to put my life back together, he was experiencing difficulties of his own. It was in the months that we started to become friends that we joined forces and saved one another. He needed my light, and I needed his. Today we have an incredibly special partnership, that has laid out a strong foundation for our future together. I know that when we start a family of our own, it will not only be life-changing, it will be unlike anything we've ever experienced together.

Life is going to deliver us experiences, challenges, hardships and the like to help us grow. At times it won't seem fair, or just. Know that even the darkest of nights are welcomed by the coming of the early morning dawn. Find your silver lining, it's there. I promise.

Acknowledgements: I would like to thank the Universe for presenting me with experiences that continue to help me grow and step into the person I am destined to become. To my partner Jesse, my soul sisters, and the many incredible people who have come into my life since 2013, I wouldn't be here without your love and support.

About the Author

Olivia Shwetz grew up in west-central Alberta in the small town of Hinton, along the gateway to the magnificent Rocky Mountain landscape. As a child she would run barefoot around her family's acreage home, enjoying dirt covered carrots and fresh green peas from her grandparents' garden. Her sister, Lyndsay, and she would lose several hammers over the years building forts in the woods on the family property. Her friends describe her as effervescent, and a source of constant happiness. Olivia knows what struggle feels like and has experienced an array of life lessons that have gifted her with the ability to find the silver lining in all of life's experiences. She has grieved, celebrated, cried, fought, laughed, and surrendered to it all with a grateful heart. She is a woman who has walked many paths, but it was only when she stepped into her divine truth that her journey took on new meaning. By deliberately choosing to stand in her authenticity, she gives power back to thousands of women by showing them that the path back to themselves does not exist out in the world, but rather it lies within. She guides women back to their true intuitive nature with compassion, because she believes that every woman is meant to live life as her most authentic self. She believes that everyone has a wildness to them that is worth embracing.

www.wakethewildwithin.com

IG: @wakethewildwithin

FB: @wakethewildwithin

RESILIENCE

It is expected of us, that when we are shown some sort of evidence of a dismal future that we are to accept it and find a way to live with it. Resilience tells us otherwise. Resilience is the strength of our inner spirit refusing to settle for what we have been given. The human spirit only knows hope and it is what helps us get back up to fight, when everything else in our mind and body is telling us to just give in and fold. Resilience encourages us to look deeper, to peel back another layer, and to be curious about what's possible.

Margot's story shows us how possible it is for us to come back as many times as we need until we have regained our own physical health, mental stability and emotional strength. It illustrates the power of expression, communication and release, because when we choose to hold it all inside, we can bring some of our greatest nightmares into form right in front of us, and in Margot's case, within our own bodies.

EMOTIONS, THE UNCOMFORTABLE TRUTH

"Closing myself off to the pain, closed me off from feeling everything.
And in order for me to truly heal, I needed to feel it all."

−Margot Gaudet

CHAPTER THIRTEEN

Emotions, the

Uncomfortable Truth

"Well, let's start with the good news. You don't have cancer."

Dr. Weston was the neurologist assigned to my case since September 2013, when my head and face had gone numb for no reason. He was an older man, tall and slim except for his big Santa Claus belly. His bald head was shining under the artificial lights. "The bad news is, you have Multiple Sclerosis. Your spinal tap results came back positive. I'm sorry to have to tell you this."

With that news, I tuned out the rest of the doctor's words. There was no way to hold back the tears that were flooding my eyes. I felt like time had stopped, like my world as I knew it was ending. A few weeks prior to this appointment, I had woken up one morning with no feelings in most of my body. Everything from the neck down was numb mixed with very little muscle function. It had been one of the scariest things I had ever experienced. My mind was fully functional, yet it was like someone had switched bodies on me.

My partner, who was working out of province, came home early to be with me. Although he sat by my side, I still felt completely alone. Unlike me, he has never been an affectionate person. And at that time, affection and the kind of support that only an intimate partner can provide to a person, are what I needed the most. Despite the dismal news of my diagnosis, I had secretly hoped this would be the thing that brought us closer. I was secretly hoping that it would be the catalyst that would bring more physical and emotional intimacy in our relationship. But it did the opposite.

Roughly one year prior to this appointment, I had been hospitalized after suffering a heart attack, that the doctors discovered was brought on by Addison's Disease. Three weeks later, I was hospitalized for Congestive Heart Failure. I feel like I navigated through most of that with barely anyone by my side. My parents were gone on vacation, so was my best friend, and my partner was working out of town. That day in the doctor's office, facing another devastating diagnosis, I was hoping this would be what would finally bring us closer.

The doctor stepped out and left us with the nurse. My partner was now speaking with her, asking all sorts of questions for me that I couldn't seem to articulate. Most of them were met with the same answer: "We don't know." Not being able to get most of the questions answered made the news even harder to bear. There were so many unknowns, and so much fear. How was I ever going to make it through this? I felt like I was spiraling out of control down a black hole of despair, all the while my mind was screaming "why me?" Had I not been through enough?

The following months pushed me far beyond anything I had ever experienced. It had been extremely difficult not personally knowing anyone with MS who I could talk to, to help ease my fears. The nurse had also cautioned me about joining any online groups that could so often be filled with even more dread and toxicity. Weeks were spent lying hopelessly on the couch watching the world go by. I wanted so desperately to participate in life again, but it felt so completely inaccessible to me. It was like watching from someone else's body with no control over anything.

Family and friends were continually showing up with all their love and support during the first few months and with that, often came advice. Their advice came from their hearts, yet I would still find myself feeling empty and frustrated.

"Just think positive!"

"Keep listing things you're grateful for every day!"

"Everything happens for a reason."

"It could be much worse."

In my mind I knew all of that, but I was still paralyzed beyond my new physical limitations. I was stuck in fear, anger and bitterness. There were unmet needs crying to be acknowledged. All of these unprocessed emotions were trumping my ability to feel anything remotely close to gratitude. I was trying to count my blessings between clenched teeth and it wasn't working for me.

My dear friends and family were doing their best to support me out of love, but what was hurting me the most was the lack of connection with my partner. I felt this time of crisis should have brought us closer together, when instead it was tearing me apart beyond anything I could have imagined. It was causing more pain and suffering than the diseases were.

I remember one night in June, about six weeks into this ordeal. A little bit of feeling had returned to my body, but I was still not sleeping more than a few hours a night. My partner was lying next to me in deep sleep. I was jealous; I could not wait to find deep, sound sleep again. My chest was still gripped by the feeling that someone was tightening a leather belt around it, a common side effect of the disease. I could barely breathe, it felt like my chest was going to collapse on me and there was no sign of it easing off. Part of me was wondering how I could feel so damn lonely when there was someone lying right next to me. But then I wondered, how could I connect with anyone when I could not even connect with my own body? As I laid there in my bed looking out the window, the full moon was casting its soft glow on the barns and everything else that was underneath it. The scene was beautiful and it was calling me. I dragged myself out of bed and all the way outside, wearing only a t-shirt and underwear as I couldn't be bothered with the rest. It was 3am after all. I went close to the fence where the horses, sheep, goats and alpacas were gathered to eat. I laid down on the cool gravel and gazed up at the moon and a few bright stars. So much beauty. The sounds of the animals feeding, mostly rhythmic chewing with the occasional gurgles and spitting from the alpacas, was soothing for me. It felt like mother nature was holding her arms around me that night. There I lay half naked in the dirt, in a complete state of vulnerability, and for the first time in ages, a sense of gratitude washed over me. I felt like I was contemplating rather than worrying. What was this experience trying to teach me? How long was this going to last? Why did I feel so lonely when I was surrounded by friends and family on a regular basis? Was this how I wanted to spend the rest of my life? What could I do about it? What did I need to do to regain my power? As the moon shone its light of hope down on me, it was like it was telling me that everything was going to be okay, and through this beautiful connection with Mother Nature herself, I allowed myself to believe it.

Long, seemingly endless weeks turned into months and around the four-month mark, some of the numbness slowly started to dissipate. After the fifth month, only my chest, hands and toes remained numb. My life slowly returned to normal, at least what would be my new normal. On my journey through recovery, I picked up a few books about MS. I was careful to choose books like: The Wahls Protocol; How I Beat Progressive MS, by Terry Wahls, M.D. and Healing Multiple Sclerosis by Ann

Boroch, CNC. There are many books on the subject of MS, but most of them are on how people have learned to live with it. That is where I made the personal decision to immerse myself in the books that focused on healing, instead of just accepting my fate and learning to live with it. I had to, as some nights I would pray that I didn't wake up the next morning. Needing help to get dressed, to wash myself, to eat and not being able to go to the washroom myself, had not been what I had envisioned for my life at 35!

A small step I took that turned into an amazing healing process for me was to start taking yoga classes. A year after the diagnosis, most of the numbness had gone, but I was now left with painful muscle spasms. Just bending my legs to sit would turn into an excruciating ordeal that most of the time left me in tears. Yoga classes were a challenge at first, because even though I had once been flexible, most of the classes in the first few weeks were spent in Shavasana (corpse pose) because the pain was just too much. But I kept going, five classes a week to be exact! Within months, I had regained my former flexibility and could participate in a full class like everyone else. I was no longer experiencing any muscles spasms. I had not had a headache in months and mentally I was in a much better place. The classes were also helping me to socialize again in an intimate and safe way.

Becoming aware of how I was speaking about the illnesses I was dealing with also produced positive changes for me. Months after the MS diagnosis, I became aware that when I was speaking about it, I had been referring to it as My MS. As soon as I became aware of this, I knew I had to change it because I no longer wanted to hang onto it, by identifying myself with it. Once I started to see some physical progress, I was able to regain some mental clarity and calm my fears. This allowed me to start focusing on my emotional health, which I believe to be the root of my decline in health in the first place. I was just so exhausted from holding everything in so that I would look strong and not make anyone uncomfortable. In life we rarely learn about emotional health, so when someone is genuinely expressing their emotions, we tend to shy away because their emotions make us feel uncomfortable. We have so much work to do around emotions and how to express them, feel through them, and release them in a healthy and safe way. It's my belief and experience that if we can't do this, our emotions come to rest in our bodies and physiologically manifest themselves in the form of illness. I have also learned how my deep feelings of loneliness made my experience that much more painful. It magnified every insecurity and every fear. It made me feel incredibly small, and only accelerated my already rapid decline in self-confidence. With more reading and research, I had also realized that I was using the illnesses as crutches or excuses for all the things I had stopped doing in my life, like the dreams I had stopped chasing and the effort I had stopped putting into my projects. It was like having these beautiful balloons of hope and someone would come along with a giant pin and pop them, only I was the person with the pin. Instead of taking ownership of my goals, the moment I would face a challenge, I would blame the illness. Pop!

Yet even with all these empowering discoveries about my life, I still found myself feeling empty inside most of the time. I was still laughing with friends, but it didn't feel like it came from deep down inside. The spark in my life had disappeared. I would often wonder if I would ever truly, deeply feel again. Or would I stay numb and empty forever? It's true what they say, that the answers we seek are already within us. I knew that in order to thrive, I had to look deep inside; deeper than I had ever cared to, or allowed myself to, look before. I started working on my inner blocks and limiting belief systems by journaling my reflections on feelings and experiences. I started doing EFT (emotional freedom technique) sessions and, within months, a huge revelation emerged. I have been feeling so much emptiness, because I have been disconnected from my own sense of sensuality. The realization left me in tears for days in an odd mix of sadness and relief. It wasn't the sexual form of sensuality that I was craving, it was about living every day in a way that was going to fuel my soul. I had spent so much of my life working to please others and ignoring my own needs, only to wind up riddled with illnesses. I then turned all of my attention on how not to be ill. I had to discover my own desires. What did Margot desire?

I desired to travel, to eat delicious foods, to have deep soulful conversations with people, to connect with my creativity and allow myself to dream again. Those things are what make life sensual for me and I had totally disconnected from them because I was too busy giving all my time, thoughts and energy to my illnesses. I made a decision for myself, out of love, that I would reconnect with my soul, reconnect with my body and reconnect with my passion and joy for life. I made the decision that I want to thrive in the face of illness. This realization is my new guidepost for my future. To make decisions in my life that lead me closer to that which I desire and spark a sense of deep, authentic joy. I let myself dream, no matter how impossible it may seem.

In February 2019, I travelled to the Dominican Republic. I ate delicious food, and engaged in deep soulful conversations with a few people I met while I was there. I embraced life fully as my able body danced the night away with the sand between my toes, a smile on my face and the deepest feelings of gratitude for the life that I get to live. My sensual life, that I choose to live.

This trip showed me but a glimpse of what is possible in my life when I tap into my deepest desires in life. When I truly participate in the things that bring me joy, like traveling, soulful conversations, time in nature and amazing food, it lights me up, it feeds my soul and regenerates my health. It does for me what no amount of medication can do. It's true healing at its core, it's not drugs to cover up symptoms of a life unlived.

Acknowledgements: I'd like to thank my parents for their love and support throughout my life, as well as my partner, family and friends. You've all helped me become the woman I am today.

About the Author

Margot Gaudet was born and raised in a small, rural New Brunswick village, surrounded by rolling hills, beautiful farmland and wide-open skies. Growing up on a dairy farm is what nurtured Margot's unwavering love and respect for nature and animals. Since childhood, she has been fiery, fierce and passionate about what matters to her. Margot's life came crashing down when she was 34 years old. She suffered a heart attack, was diagnosed with Addison's Disease, Lyme Disease, Multiple Sclerosis and Thyroid cancer, all within 22 months. This journey through ill health has amplified her longtime dreams of creating a healing space where coaches and teachers can bring small, intimate groups together to connect with nature, animals and themselves. Margot founded Maven Hill

Farm in 2018, and she is now working on adding a guest house for workshop participants, as well as adding gardens and a small orchard on the property, to share her love of fresh homegrown food with others. She is extremely proud of the energy she has infused on her small farm. Having studied in hospitality and tourism, biodynamic farming, and permaculture design, and getting certified as an autopoetic facilitator, have helped shape her vision for a healing and gathering space. Margot made a decision to dedicate herself to her own personal development, which has been instrumental in her physical and emotional healing. Margot has the ability to savor life at its core, she loves deeply and dreams big.

www.mavenhillfarm.com

IG: @mavenhillfarm

FB @mavenhillfarm

email: margot@mavenhillfarm.com

CONVICTION

If we don't do all things with absolute and total conviction, are we really trying our best? Conviction is the deep belief that the path we choose is exactly where we are meant to be, despite it not being the easy or popular choice. It is the tenacious grit in pursuit of what is both right for, and in alignment with, your soul. Conviction is what gives fuel to our heart space to keep going, when the going gets tough. It is what locks our eyes on our destination and signs a contract with our soul to depart on the journey and commit to seeing it through.

In the conclusion to this compilation of soul touching stories, Sarah shares the birth story of The Great Canadian Woman, and how She exists in every woman across Canada, because The Great Canadian Woman is all of us.

THE GREAT CANADIAN WOMAN

"She makes waves. She moves mountains.
And she blazes trails."

–Sarah Swain

CHAPTER FOURTEEN

The Great Canadian Woman

It was February of 2018 as I packed my bags, eager to feel the warm California sun on my face, and the sand between my toes. I had taken a leave of absence from my job in November, desperately needing to reassess my life and the direction I wanted it to move in. I had climbed the corporate ladder rather quickly. As a woman in my early thirties, I never allowed my age or my gender to be a reason to slow me down, or hold me back, despite the unconscious gender bias that existed all around me in the corporate world. However, the lifestyle filled with hotels, board rooms, airport lounges and countless nights away from home eventually caught up to me, leaving me wondering if I had missed the point entirely. Is this it? Is this what we live for? I was tired of living for the weekends, and having mid-week date nights with my husband over Face-time. None of it made sense to me anymore, and it left me questioning everything. In January, when my leave expired, I made a decision not to return to work, with nothing more than a business idea floating around in my mind and a fire burning in my belly. My Soul took the wheel in what felt like a momentary lapse of courage and said, this isn't how we are going to live this life. It's now or never. I walked away from my six-figure salary, and just in case I felt the urge to run back to safety, I emptied my closet of my corporate clothes, threw them into bags and gave them all away to women in the workforce! Burn the boats. These words played over and over in my mind, passed onto me from a former mentor. I figured, if I had a moment of weakness and begged for my job back, I would have to do it naked. I felt strong and confident in my bold, yet slightly irrational decision, as my husband, Rob, watched on in horror.

(Q

As the plane touched down at LAX, I could feel a stir within me. I knew this weekend had something big in store, I just didn't know what. I was eager to attend The Bliss Project, hosted by Lori Harder , someone I admire greatly in life and business. They say you're drawn to those who embody what you desire to have and become yourself, and Lori had been that person for me for years. First on the agenda, I hopped into my rental car, and typed in the words 'Venice Beach" and started driving as I could feel some of the cold rigidity of my nervous system begin to thaw. I pulled into the beach parking lot, and the view of the Pacific was blocked by a large sand embankment. I frantically stuck some money in the parking meter as my feet were aching to hit the warm sand and my eyes were equally eager to see the water. Alberta winters are no joke, but this one had been particularly tough as I fought my way through the trials and tribulations of starting a business and recreating my life at the age of 32. I was desperate to get to the water and begin to feel a sense of calm for the first time in months. Like a car that had its gaslight on for the last 50 kms, I needed to refuel quickly and water is my gasoline. I paid for my parking and jogged towards the embankment, momentarily wondering how Canadian I must have looked as my sun-deprived body awkwardly fumbled its way through the sand like it had never experienced a warm beach before. The breeze hit me hard as my head popped over the top and I took in the beauty of the ocean before me. With my flip-flops in hand, I headed straight for her. The moment my toes hit the water, I felt myself breathe for the first time since I left my job. It was the first time I felt a sense of peace wash over me, and a sudden reassurance that I wasn't crazy or irresponsible for choosing a different way to live. It was moments like this one that reminded me that life didn't need to be as hard as we had made it out to be. It really could be filled with joy, peace and calm, and we have the power to make it so.

(Q

You're Canadian?! Omg me too! Where are you from?! Is that near Toronto? Omg I've always wanted to see the East Coast! British Columbia is stunning! Yes, I got married in the Canadian Rockies! I'm in Alberta, too! What a small world! I know, I know – it's a tiny town and you'll miss it on the Trans Canada if you blink. Yes, only one set of lights in my hometown! Eh?! I don't have an accent, you have an accent! Everywhere I turned all weekend, it felt like I was bumping into Canadians. And you know what happens when a Canadian finds another Canadian while in another country: instant connection! It was both incredible and intriguing that so many of us had been drawn to one single event. The Canadian pride could be felt throughout the room, as we all felt proud to tell everyone exactly where we were from.

As the weekend came to an end, I offered to give a ride to a couple of the attendees who were looking to get back to LAX to catch their Sunday evening flights. We all piled into the car and introduced ourselves formally after we buckled up. We quickly found ourselves laughing as we exchanged introductions in the car, discovering that all three of us were Canadian. Of course! Quelle surprise! I spent my flight back to Edmonton reflecting on the weekend, feeling a renewed sense of confidence in the direction I had chosen to take, even though I had no idea the monumental shift in direction that awaited.

The thought of all of the Canadian women in California felt like it was hanging out on my shoulder nearly every day since returning, like I had become subconsciously obsessed with this phenomenon. In my office, which I commonly referred to as The Lady Cave, were all kinds of white boards covered in post-it notes. I'm a visual person, and absorb information the best when I can see it boldly before me. June 30th was a date written on one of the bright pieces of paper. It was the deadline I had given myself to launch a podcast. Truthfully, I stuck the date up there just to keep me accountable, as at the time I had no clarity on what it would even be about. As I continued to take leaps in my business throughout the spring, June 30th kept staring me in the face. Not executing something when I said I would simply isn't in my DNA, so I was beginning to feel a little anxious about my lack of clarity. What the heck was it going to be about?

The podcast needs to be for Canadian women. It came to me as a whisper one day. What does that mean? I entered into a conversation within my own mind as the message continued to download. It came pouring in faster and faster as it all started to click together.

So many Canadian women are doing really powerful things with their lives yet so many of us don't know about them. Why? There are so many of us, yet we are all so far apart. So many Canadian women have businesses that other Canadian women need, but don't know about. Imagine if the product or service you needed was right in your community? What if someone in Nova Scotia could reach a woman in Saskatchewan and positively impact her life by sharing a piece of her story? What if the event that someone was holding in Vancouver could bring in people from Ontario and Quebec? We just need to know about it! Canadians are proud people. Strong. Resilient. Brilliant. Kind. Heart centred! There are so many women here making waves! Why don't we know more about them?! Where is the platform?! The platform.

This whirlwind of a mental download had me feeling both excited and terrified, with an entire spectrum of emotions in between. The imposter known as self-doubt showed up in my mind immediately. Who do you think you are? Who are you to create a space for, and represent Canadian Women? Shaking it off, I looked up at the fluorescent sticky note. June 30th. Holy crap...July 1st, the very next day – Canada Day. Make it happen.

The coming weeks had me flooded with excitement, that would then become superseded by fear, and I would roll around in this cycle as my Soul fought for me to stay focused on what I had been called to create. I was chatting with my sister Amanda one day over text, and had filled her in on my big idea. I also expressed to her my fear of taking on the brand name, The Great Canadian Woman.

"Why?" she asked.

"It feels like a really huge responsibility, and I don't know if I have what it takes." I responded.

"What would you say to me about fear if I were in your shoes?" she rebutted.

"Well played, Sister." I replied as I hit the send button.

From that moment forward, it was decided. The Great Canadian Woman was going to enter into this world, and I was merely going to be her gracious host. On July 1, 2019, The Great Canadian Woman podcast was launched, and her beautiful community began to form.

The Great Canadian Woman makes waves, she moves mountains and she blazes trails. She also knocks me off my feet on a daily basis in a state of complete awe and admiration. The women who raise their hand and show up with courage to share a piece of their life, for the sole purpose of helping another Canadian woman, has been one of the most humbling experiences I have ever had in my entire life. What had started out as an idea to help Canadian women connect and come to know one another, rapidly turned into a full-fledged movement. The original concept of a monthly guest episode on the podcast quickly changed to weekly, as applications began to pour in from women all across Canada, eager to have a space to share their stories, businesses, expertise and insight with the Canadian marketplace. It was working. Women were connecting, businesses were being born, services were being shared, collaborations were in the works and new friends were being made. Holy crap, it's working! In an act of sheer alignment, my brand new baby business as I knew it, rebranded itself entirely as The Great Canadian Woman, and took on a life force of her own.

One of the most profound moments to date, that reaffirmed the true mission of The Great Canadian Woman was airing an episode with Brenda Wiese, now an author in this very publication. The episode went viral, as men and women alike tuned in to receive even a shred of hope that their own journey through grief and loss was survivable. Brenda's story granted them permission to survive, to be okay, and to lead a life from a place of joy. The episode was later featured on the Victims of Homicide website, as an official resource for members of their community, showcasing the highest purpose of The Great Canadian Woman Community. Brenda's story is just one of countless examples of just how connected and supported we all truly are, when we find the courage to stand up and stand out.

The Great Canadian Woman is all of us. She is the single mother who provides for her children come hell or high water. She is the woman who has a dream, and musters up enough courage to go after it. She is the woman who has quarreled in the depths of pain and grief and finds her way back home to herself. She is the woman who says no to what does not serve her. She is the woman who says enough is enough, and commits to a new way of living. She is the woman who finds the strength to leave toxic relationships. She is the woman who takes the lead and lights the torch. She is the woman who refuses to accept the limits that someone else placed before her. She is the woman who knocks on doors, and shatters glass ceilings. She is the woman who finds a way out of no way and turns around, extends her hand, and brings as many people as she can along with her.

The women who have shared their sacred stories in this book are warriors of light. They are some of the strongest and most resilient women I have ever encountered, and I know their stories represent millions across Canada. I am humbled by their courageous journeys. They exemplify what it means to be The Great Canadian Woman, Strong and Free. Their voices give hope to other women, that they too can change the trajectory of their lives, if the course they are travelling doesn't serve them. Their expertise and insight inspire women to make better choices for themselves and take empowered action towards their lives with intention. Their stories grant us all the permission to live fully, love deeply and to fight like hell in the name of truth and joy. I am so proud of you. Thank you for being the foundation of this incredible platform, as you lead the way for women all across Canada.

If you know you are on the verge of something beautiful in your life, I want to leave you with this. You can, and you will. Embody the vision you have for yourself. Become it by surrounding yourself with who and what aligns, and hit the pause button on anything that doesn't. Stand for yourself, for your mission and your purpose with such conviction that even the most devastating storm can't shake your foundation. Become unstoppable in your pursuit of joy, bliss and freedom by taking radical ownership of your journey. Own it all. The highs, the lows, the ups, the downs, the wins, the losses, the love and the fear. There is greatness calling you forward, and it is your time. You deserve to feel strong and free.

Acknowledgement: To all Canadian women making waves, moving mountains and blazing trails. Thank you for your courage. To my Mom and Dad for your unwavering support. To my husband, Rob, for standing beside me and to my sister, Amanda, for seeing to it that I didn't let fear hold me back on this journey.

About the Author

Born and raised in the small town of Massey, Ontario, Sarah Swain transitioned into adulthood in the big city of Toronto before heading west with her husband, Rob, to wed in the Canadian Rocky Mountains and start their life together in the prairies. Now residing on the east coast, you can find Sarah beachcombing in the summer, and snowshoeing in the winter in one of Canada's most untapped nature playgrounds – New Brunswick. Always excited about the idea of exploring, Sarah is eager for adventure in Canada, which means she knows there is still another cross country move in her yet.

Sarah is the Founder and Director of The Great Canadian Woman Inc. She saw a need for a deeper sense of connection amongst Canadian women, despite the physical distance between us. Starting out as a podcast, it quickly grew into a multi-faceted platform designed for Canadian women to share their stories, insight, businesses and expertise with the Canadian marketplace. The Great Canadian Woman Podcast was one of fifty podcasts chosen to be featured by Apple iTunes as part of their Inspiring Women campaign on International Women's Day 2019.

Stepping into the world of entrepreneurship was inevitable for Sarah, as she has a natural gift for seeing how things can be executed more powerfully, more efficiently and with more heart. Unmanageable is often how she was respectfully described by her leaders, as she climbed the ladder at lightning speed, challenging the powers that be with every step. Yet deep down, Sarah knew there was more to be had and experienced in life, and in 2017 she committed to exploring that thought, no matter what. Taking action on building her dreams before she felt ready for it, is one of Sarah's greatest pieces of advice for new entrepreneurs. Just start.

www.thegreatcanadianwoman.ca

IG: @thegreatcanadianwoman

FB: @thegreatcanadianwoman

Final Words

As The Great Canadian Woman brand and platform continues to grow, it is our mission to represent all Canadian women no matter what creed, background, sexual orientation, physical form, mental state, race or origin. Whether your roots in Canada reach back for centuries, or you are a newly-landed immigrant, know there is a place in this community for you. In order to continue reaching women all across Canada, we need your help. Please share this book with a loved one, connect deeper with the authors and help spread their stories. Through our differences, no matter how large or small, there will always exist a sense of interconnectedness that bridges us all. Please follow along at www.thegreatcanadianwoman.ca and watch for future publishing, blog, event and podcast opportunities.

Credit Notes

Calgary Homicide Support Society

http://calgaryhss.ca/

Canadian Veterans Affairs - PTSD Awareness
https://www.veterans.gc.ca/eng/health-support/mental-health-and-wellness/understanding-mental-health/ptsd-warstress

Canadian Mental Health Association

https://cmha.ca/

Edmonton Victims of Homicide Support Society

http://www.victimsofhomicide.org/

The Bliss Project by Lori Harder

https://www.loriharder.com/events/bliss-project/